BRITAIN'S ARMED FORCES TODAY:1

RAF STRIKE COMMAND

Paul Jackson

LONDON
IAN ALLAN LTD

CONTENTS

First published 1984

ISBN 0 7110 1437 X

Published by Ian Allan Ltd, Shepperton, Surrey; and printed by Ian Allan Printing Ltd at their works at Coombelands in Runnymede, England.

INTRODUCTION

When Strike Command was established in 1968, it inherited the traditions of two previous Royal Air Force formations whose role in the defence of freedom is acknowledged throughout the world. The successors of Fighter and Bomber Commands formed a firm basis on which to build the RAF's single home-based operational Command, and in later years this force was swelled by maritime, offensive support and transport units.

Today, Strike Command is the operator of all the types of RAF aircraft with which Britain would go to war, its weaponry ranging from machine guns to tactical nuclear weapons. Other aircraft perform the vital but often unsung tasks of transport and communications, whilst SAR helicopters undertake their missions of mercy. Until recently, it seemed that Strike Command would remain largely a European force, but the Falklands war — in which it performed with distinction — has resulted in an extended overseas presence and participation in a front-line situation as demanding as that of its companion, RAF Germany.

But the Command does not exist solely for national purposes. For a decade, Strike Command has had the NATO title of United Kingdom Air Forces to reflect its complete commitment to the Alliance at any time Europe is under threat. Regular air exercises and squadron interchanges reinforce the bond between airmen of different but like-minded nations and serve notice to potential adversaries of the West's determination to be left in peace. Strike Command is neither the largest nor smallest air combat force dedicated to NATO, but its claim to be the best is not easily refuted.

'Defend and Strike': the motto incorporated in the badge of Royal Air Force Strike Command is brief, yet amply descriptive of its role. Combining all front-line elements outside RAF Germany, the Command is charged with defending Britain, its possessions and friends from enemy attack and striking an aggressor's armed forces and their supply organisations — tasks which the Service and its predecessors have undertaken with courage and determination in two world wars and numerous smaller conflicts and confrontations. Trained to what is acknowledged by many as the highest standard in the world, Strike Command represents the most vital component of Britain's armed forces: a comprehensive, mobile and adaptable arm, effective over land and sea as well as in its own element.

These many facets of the Command imply its operation of a wide variety of aircraft and armament, and as such, it is unique in the history of the RAF. The effectiveness and cost of modern weapons, allied to political reductions in Britain's overseas commitments, have resulted in a considerable diminution in the RAF's size compared even with two decades ago. Previously, the RAF Commands specialised in one function only — Bomber, Fighter, Transport, etc — and they were further sub-divided into groups and their component squadrons, but such has been the contraction, that now one group is sufficient to adminster the aircraft and men formerly comprising a command. Thus, in 1968, just 50 years after its formation from the Royal Flying Corps and Royal Naval Air Service, the RAF began a process of reorganisation and amalgamation which has resulted in the integration of eight commands into a mere two.

Today's Strike Command perpetuates the roles and honours of the now dissolved Bomber, Fighter, Coastal and Transport Commands; whilst its companion Support Command controls the functions of the former Flying Training, Technical Training, Maintenance and Signals Commands. A separate organisation, RAF Germany, represents the forward spearhead of British air power in Europe, sharing many of its

Above:
Strike Command's nerve-centre is in the village of Naphill, immediately north of High Wycombe, Buckinghamshire. As evidenced by the NATO flag flying alongside the Union Jack, Strike Command is declared to the Alliance as United Kingdom Air Forces. *HQSC*

front-line aircraft with Strike Command. By the end of 1983, 'Strike' had been slimmed to a three-group formation, representing a mere fraction of the units which had once been subordinate to its predecessors.

The genesis of today's structure may be traced to 14 July 1936 and the simultaneous establishment of Bomber, Fighter and Coastal Commands as the framework on which an expanding air force was to be built to counter the threat of German military aspirations. As each of these commands was equipped from the growing pace of British rearmament, component groups were formed — normally in reserved numerical ranges — to administer several stations and their resident squadrons. For Bomber Command, the process began on 20 March 1936 with the formation of No 2 Group, and by the end of 1937 five such units were in being to administer the forces with which the RAF went to war in September 1939.

No 1 Group (formed 1 May 1936) flew its Fairey Battle light bombers to France to reinforce the Armée de l'Air, becoming the HQ Advanced Air Striking Force in the process, and after a comparatively quiet winter, its aircraft suffered terrible casualties in the German blitzkrieg of May and June 1940. Operating in the face of superior forces and in the absence of a co-ordinated plan of defence, the Battles were involved in desperate raids which vainly attempted to stem the Wehrmacht's inexorable advance. Considerably reduced, No 1 Group returned to Britain, where it was re-established at Bawtry Hall near Doncaster in July 1941. This was to remain its headquarters until 1983.

Bomber Command gathered further strength as the 'Expansion Plan' aircraft gave way to the four-engined 'Heavies' which took the offensive well into German territory. Aug-

Above left:
Royal Air Force Strike Command.

Above:
United Kingdom Air Forces. Since April 1975, Strike Command has been declared to NATO as UK Air Forces, the insignia appropriately comprising Strike Command's badge superimposed on the NATO star.

Left:
Sir David Craig KCB, OBE, MA, RAF, was appointed Air Officer Commanding-in-Chief, Strike Command in September 1982. Born in 1929, he flew Meteors, Hunters and Vulcans and was Station Commander at the RAF College, Cranwell and at Akrotiri, Cyprus, before more recent appointments as Assistant Chief of Air Staff (Operations), AOC No 1 Group and Vice-Chief of Air Staff. *HQSC*

menting the sturdy Wellington and unhappy Manchester twins were the Stirling, Halifax and reliable Lancaster, the last-mentioned proving to be the most tractable heavy bomber of the war. January 1943 saw a further development in the Command when No 6 Group was formed to control the growing number of Canadian bomber units sharing the nightly battle against AA guns and fighters over Germany and occupied Europe; but Bomber Command's most famed subordinate was undoubtedly No 8 Group, also established in January 1943. Universally known as the Pathfinder Force, No 8 Group comprised highly trained airmen whose responsibility it was to lead the main force accurately to its target, ensuring maximum concentration and accuracy.

Lurking in the shadows and shunning publicity, No 100 Group came to Bomber Command in November 1943 to undertake 'Special Duties', an all-embracing title, in this case covering decoy, jamming and general defence-disruption tasks. No 2 Group had meanwhile specialised in light bombing work, notably with the Blenheim, Mitchell and versatile Mosquito, but in June 1943 it combined with Nos 83 and 84 Groups within Fighter Command to form the 2nd Tactical Air Force. Assigned to direct support of the invasion of Europe, 2nd TAF ended the war operating from European bases and ultimately became RAF Germany.

By the first year of peace, 1946, Bomber Command had been reduced to just Nos 1 and 3 Groups and was looking ahead to the development of jet bombers and British nuclear weapons. English Electric's twin-engined Canberra joined No 1 Group in 1951 to give a much-needed boost to its operational capabilities, although it was not until 1955 that the renowned trinity of V-Bombers began to enter service — initially with No 3 Group in the form of the Vickers Valiant. Vulcans joined No 1 Group and Victors also went to No 3, yet the Valiant was prematurely withdrawn with fatigue problems in 1965 and the Victor converted to the vital airborne refuelling role shortly afterwards. No 3 Group disbanded in November 1967, leaving No 1 to continue its Vulcan operations until the force was reduced to a single Vulcan K2 refuelling squadron in 1982. The low-level Buccaneer was also added to the offensive complement in 1969, this being after Bomber Command merged with its fighter equivalent to become Strike Command on 30 April 1968.

Likewise formed in July 1936, Fighter Command had originally comprised just No 11 Group (established two months earlier); the German offensive, however, forced a considerable expansion so that by the height of the Battle of Britain it controlled Nos 9-14 Groups covering the whole of the country. The Hurricane and Spitfire will forever be associated with Fighter Command in its 'finest hour', these two types of aircraft continuing to occupy a position of distinction in the RAF as evidenced by their preservation in flying condition by the Battle of Britain Memorial Flight at Coningsby. A nominal change of title to Air Defence of Great Britain between November 1943 and October 1944 heralded the arrival of jet fighters — Meteor first, then in postwar years the Vampire — and with the gradual replacement of piston-engined types, Hunters and Javelins arrived in the 1950s to shoulder the burden of defending Britain's airspace.

Fighter Command went supersonic in 1960 when English

Above:
The Lancaster epitomises Strike Command's role in World War 2 and the memory is perpetuated by the only flying example, part of the Battle of Britain Memorial Flight. *MoD*

Below:
The Falklands war showed that the RAF is as committed, as professional and as able today to wage war against Britain's enemies as it was in the past. Here the CO of No 1 Squadron, Wg Cdr Peter Squire, lands aboard HMS *Hermes* on 18 May 1982 somewhere in the South Atlantic. *Sgt Bowman*

Bottom:
The shape of things to come — the new Tornado F2 will take over the air defence role from the Lightning and part of the Phantom force in the late 1980s.

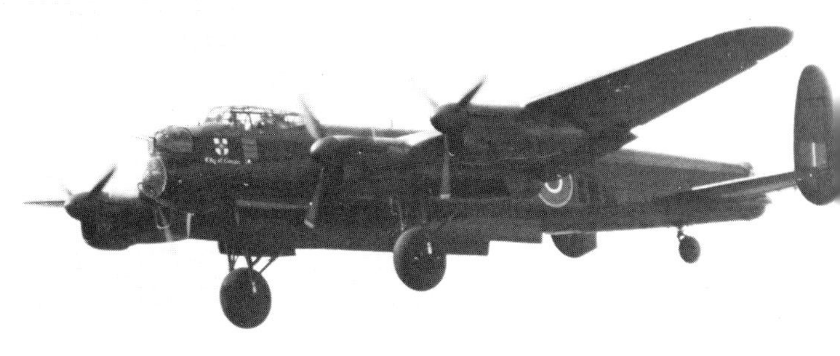

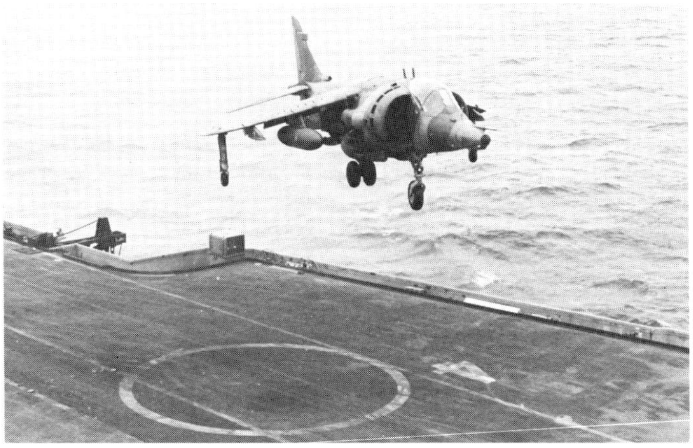

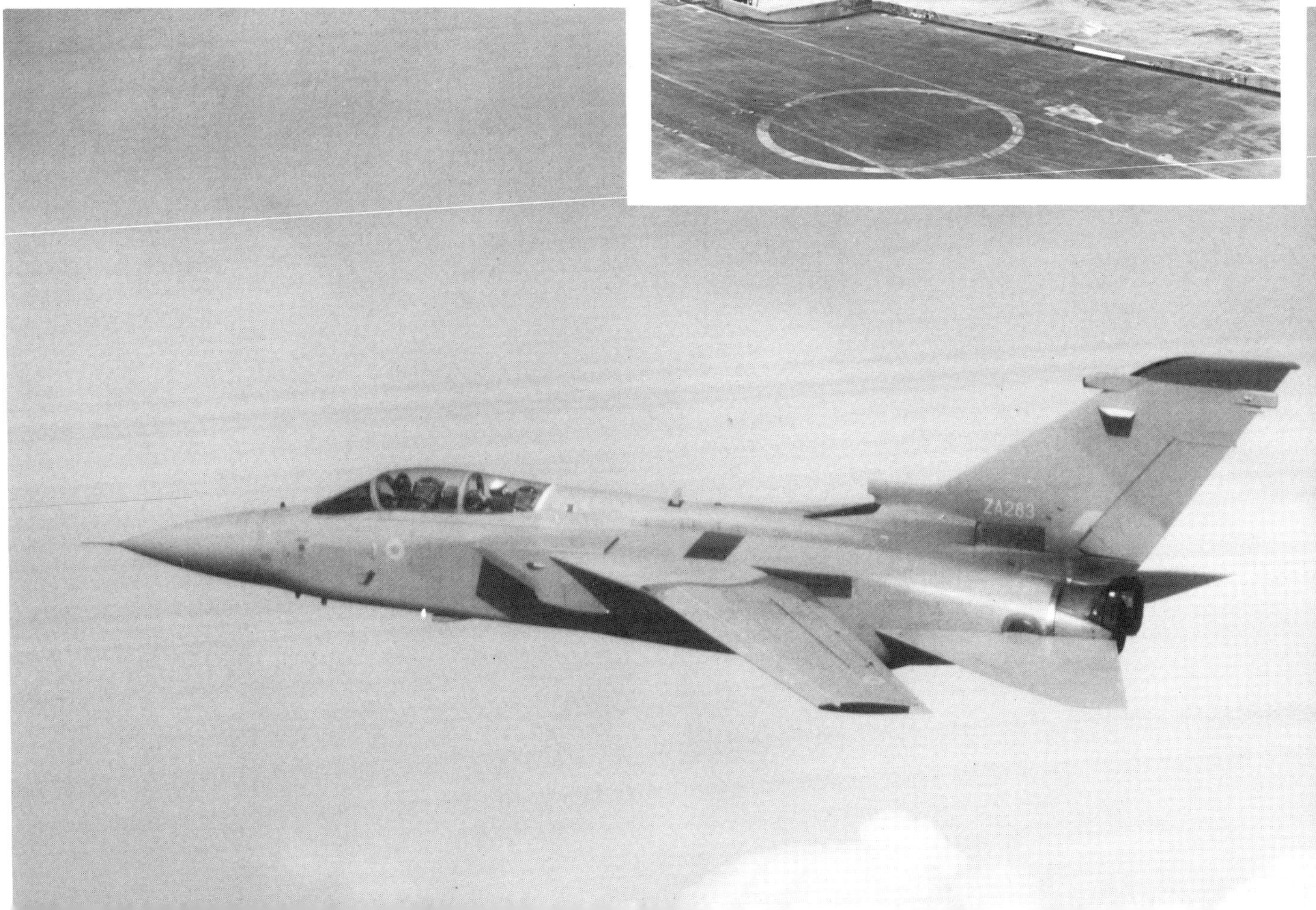

Electric Lightnings took the field, yet by the following year the two remaining groups had been reduced to sector status: No 11 at Leconfield and No 12 at Horsham St Faith. However, on 1 April 1968, the original No 11 Group returned to adminster the interceptor force, its status rapidly changing when Fighter Command became a founder member of Strike Command at the end of the same month.

As a maritime nation, Britain has traditionally attached considerable importance to defence of its sea lanes, and Coastal Command of the RAF came into being in May 1936 to survey the areas beyond the island's shores. Comprising at its peak Nos 15-19 Groups, plus the reconnaissance No 106 Group, the Command was a vital element in defeating the submarine threat to essential supply lines during World War 2, its present function differing little from the original task, save that today's missile submarines carry more destructive force than the total of ordnance exploded during the earlier conflict. An operator of long-range surveillance aircraft such as the Consolidated Liberator and Short Sunderland flying boat, Coastal Command was reduced to Nos 18 and 19 Groups in the immediate postwar period and standardised on the Avro Shackleton for its lonely patrols of the ocean's depths. During the 1950s it became responsible for helicopter-equipped SAR (Search and Rescue) flights which have now saved countless lives — civilian as well as military — and more recently has adopted the Nimrod as its principal surveillance equipment. Nos 18 and 19 Groups became Northern and Southern Maritime Air Regions when Coastal Command was merged with Strike Command on 28 November 1969, but No 18 was immediately resuscitated to become the controlling unit for all RAF maritime operations.

Transport Command was a late addition to the RAF structure, coming into being on 25 March 1943 when Ferry Command (formed 20 July 1941) was renamed. Undertaking the worldwide air supply of British bases and providing transport for airborne forces, it originally comprised Nos 44-48 Groups, plus No 38 in the Airborne role, its first postwar triumph being participation in the Berlin Airlift of 1948. Equipped with a wide variety of aircraft including the de Havilland Comet jet, introduced in 1956, the Command reflected the needs of a rapid development force by incorporating a strike-fighter element alongside the cargo and communications squadrons.

No 38 Group, the offensive support component, re-formed in January 1960 and in August 1967, together with No 46 Group's transports, became the newly titled Air Support Command. Both units joined Strike Command in September 1972, and on 1 January 1976 No 38 absorbed its companion. By this time the Group had standardised on the Hercules and VC10 for transport duties and Jaguar and Harrier for close air support. Helicopters also undertook important duties within the Group, particularly on behalf of the Army.

Finally, a brief association with Strike Command was enjoyed by the former Signals Command which came into being on 3 November 1958 to administer squadrons assigned to calibration and electronic warfare training duties. On 30 April 1968 it reverted to its former title of No 90 Group and was incorporated in Strike Command on 1 January 1969 — this arrangement lasting only until 1 May 1972 when it passed to Maintenance Command (which combined with Training Command on 1 September 1973 to form Support Command).

The foregoing, though by no means able to do justice to the richness of tradition and achievement inherent in today's Strike Command, will provide some indication of the diversity of roles entrusted to the RAF's major operational formation. Equipped for both massive destruction and the saving of human life, it is an effective and flexible force envied by others around the globe for its professionalism and efficiency and relied upon by the Army and Navy for essential support of their operations. Capable of response at speed to any threat on land, sea or in the air, Strike Command remains — as its forebears were in 1940 — Britain's first and most vital line of defence.

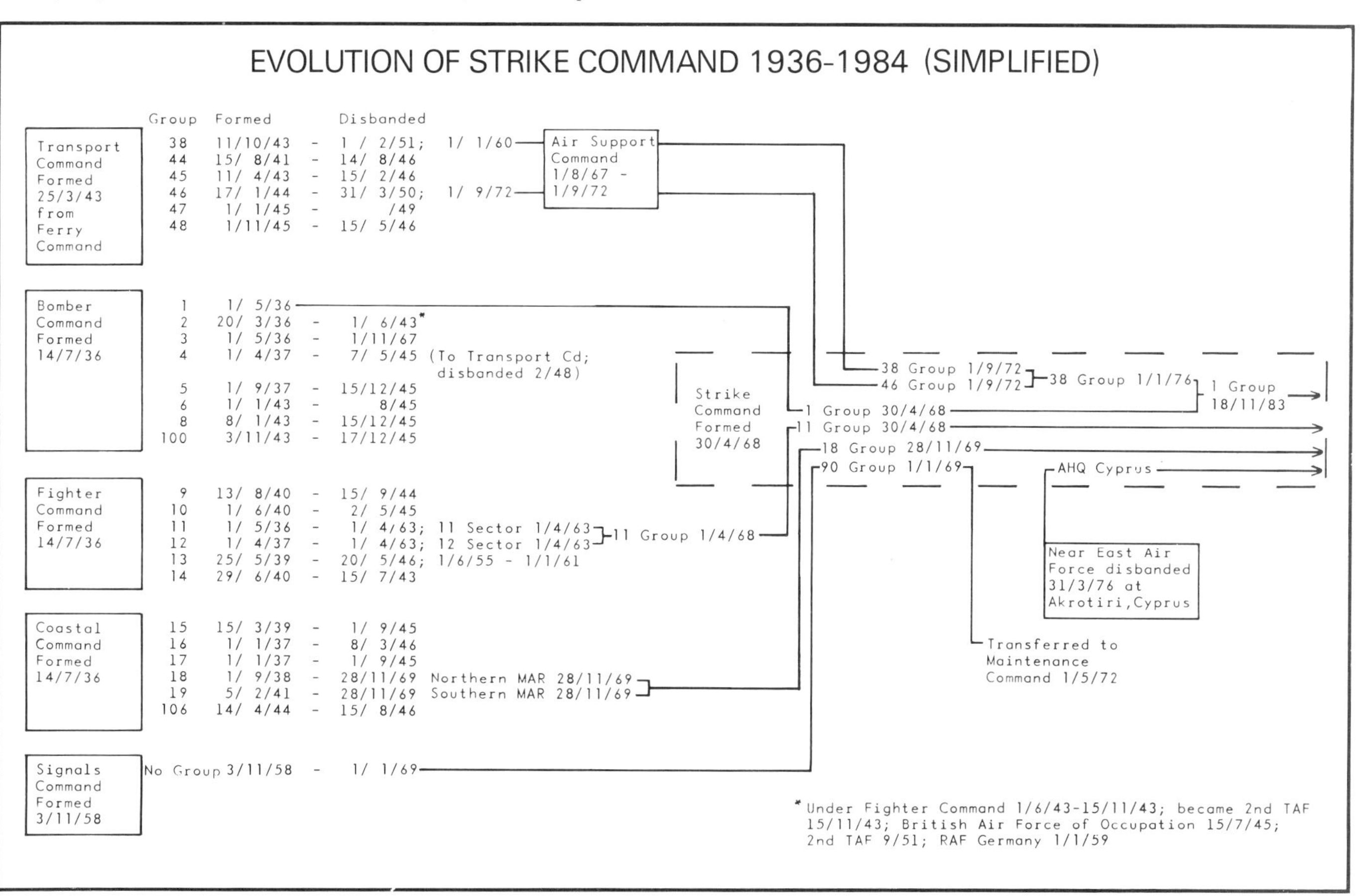

EVOLUTION OF STRIKE COMMAND 1936-1984 (SIMPLIFIED)

Embracing the full range of RAF front-line aircraft, Strike Command is charged with performing almost every operational task assigned to an air force anywhere in the world — long-range strategic nuclear attack being the principal exception since Britain's deterrent passed to the Royal Navy Polaris submarines in 1969. Briefly, the Command's tasks are: medium-range interdiction with conventional and nuclear weapons; strategic and tactical reconnaissance; airborne early warning; strategic and tactical support for all three Services; maritime reconnaissance and strike, including AS warfare; and air defence of the United Kingdom and the Fleet. The list lengthens, however, when it is remembered that many of these functions demand in-flight refuelling aircraft, SAR back-up and a comprehensive training organisation to provide personnel with the skills appropriate to their exacting roles.

Traditionally — as evidenced by its allocation to No 1 Group — the strike element has been considered of paramount importance in the RAF, not least because as an island nation, Britain's air arm would often carry the burden of attacking a land-based enemy force or naval group before the other two Services were committed. Recently, with the withdrawal of the last Vulcan B2s from the bombing task, the RAF has been denuded of long-range strike aircraft for the first time in its history ('long' of course being defined by the standards of the day). In place of the Vulcan has come the Tornado GR1, a far smaller, two-seat aircraft packed with sophisticated navigation aids which enable it to penetrate enemy defences in all weathers. Keenly welcomed by the RAF for its performance and maintainability, the Tornado has a shorter unrefuelled combat radius (850nm) compared with the 1,250nm of its predecessor and, as such, the majority of operational Tornado squadrons are being deployed by RAF Germany where they will be closer to the principal threat. This is of value in so far as reaction time is concerned, although there are other advantages accruing to the policy of maintaining one's strike forces as far back as possible from the front line. During its days as strategic deterrent vehicle the Vulcan force regularly practised dispersal to airfields throughout Britain for additional security against pre-emptive strike but a concentration of Tornados on a small number of bases would undoubtedly attract unwelcome attention.

Measures have been taken to protect the Tornado against conventional attack, with the result that its airfields are the first in Strike Command to be equipped with hardened aircraft shelters (HAS). These hangarettes of reinforced concrete with stout blast-doors will withstand a direct hit by a 1,000lb bomb and are equipped with all the facilities for 'turning-round' aircraft after a sortie. Their design has profited from experience in RAF Germany — where the HAS is a standard feature — and the UK installations are fitted for hydrant refuelling of their two resident Tornados and provision for weapon and other equipment storage in a similarly hardened annex. Aircraft may start-up engines within the HAS and taxi out for a mission under their own power, return being accomplished by an electric winch.

For maximum operational efficiency the Tornado would adopt the classic hi-lo-hi mission profile from a UK base, flying high to minimise fuel consumption until within reach of

enemy radar, then hugging the terrain to penetrate the hostile area. With the advent of 'look-down/shoot-down' weaponry which allows an interceptor to destroy a target lower than itself, this mode of attack is less secure than previously was the case, although the Tornado's extensive ECM (electronic countermeasures) equipment and its ability to fly through, rather than over, the terrain ensure that it is by no means a sitting target.

Any strike or defensive measure is only as effective as the information on which it is based, and it is for this reason that reconnaissance is an important function of Strike Command. The availability of satellites has reduced considerably the need for manned strategic reconnaissance aircraft, though the hasty conversion of flight-refuelling Victors to this role for surveillance of the South Atlantic during the Falklands war suggests that the RAF has been premature in disbanding its long-range, high-altitude recce squadrons.

In the NATO land-based context, however, the lightweight fighter-recce aircraft has an important role to play in gathering tactical information for ground and air forces, particularly in connection with the rapid thrust forward which may be expected of Soviet tank divisions in Europe. Here it is vital that enemy movements be reported as rapidly as possible in order that defensive lines may be drawn and choke-points or bottlenecks predicted for an effective air strike. With the disbandment in 1982 of the RAF's last two Canberra recce squadrons, this task will fall principally to the Jaguar, and to a lesser extent, the Harrier.

Home-based units of these aircraft might deploy to the Continent in time of war, but only one of the three Jaguar squadrons in Strike Command is tasked with reconnaissance. These aircraft carry beneath the centreline a half-ton sensor pod, which is fitted with a fan of four optical cameras for horizon-to-horizon cover and one forward-facing camera. The pod additionally includes infra-red linescan equipment which takes a 'heat picture' of the target to reveal detail which would remain hidden from more conventional means of surveillance, such as generators or engines (betraying troop presence) beneath camouflage netting, or the heat shadow left by an aircraft on the hardstanding after it has taken off.

A high degree of initiative is sought from reconnaissance pilots, who must often operate alone, rather than in formation, and provide a verbal report of their sortie to back-up the photographic evidence obtained. Film is processed at the remarkable speed of 120ft/min by mobile Reconnaissance Intelligence Centres attached to Jaguar and Harrier squadrons thus tasked, and a team of specialist photo-interpreters is on hand to examine negatives stereoscopically on a light-table before reports are dispatched with all speed to higher command.

Though the Harrier is limited in the recce role by its single port-facing camera, it is a most useful aircraft in the role of supporting ground forces — as clearly shown by the Falklands war. Requiring a short, semi-prepared take-off run in order to carry its full ordnance load — a technique known as STO/VL (short take-off and vertical landing) — the Harrier GR3 can accompany troops almost to the front line in order to speed reaction time and maximise sorties. Discounting carrier-based

Above:
Harrier at war. No 1 Squadron's Harrier GR3s were hastily fitted with provision for Sidewinder self-defence missiles during the Falklands war of 1982, and this option has been retained.
RAF Official

Below:
Puma HC1s of No 33 Squadron are allocated to both the NATO Mobile Force and its UK counterpart. A typical forward base would have woods nearby for concealment, such as this farm field. Note the polyvalent air filters fitted above the cockpit.
P. A. Jackson

Bottom:
With eight times the lifting power of the Wessex, a Chinook HC1 makes short work of a 5,000kg load of 'ammunition' (actually concrete blocks) during an exercise with the Army. The three external hooks can be used when supplies have to be delivered to different locations in a single sortie. *P. A. Jackson*

aircraft, the RAF is the only air force in the world to possess a STO/VL combat aircraft, although its capabilities for deployment are restricted by the fact the no re-supply helicopters are dedicated to the force and it remains dependent on the vagaries of road transport. For this reason, an initial wartime deployment from the UK would probably see Harriers based close to existing airfields and their ready stocks of supplies.

Accompanying Jaguars are naturally reliant on full airfield facilities — despite having demonstrated their ability to operate lightly-loaded from grass — but protection on the ground is only half the problem of minimising losses. Tasked with interdiction against targets such as vital bridges; close air support under the direction of a forward air controller (laser designation providing the key to a successful one-pass attack); and counter-air operations against enemy airfields, the Jaguar and Harrier fly low and fast to evade interception, yet faced with a determined adversary, even the best-rehearsed manoeuvring may be unable to secure their escape.

Until recently the final option was to jettison weapons and turn for home, but since the Falklands war finance has at last become available for additional defensive equipment in the form of Sidewinder air-to-air missiles. Though the strike-fighter makes no pretence of being an interceptor, the attacker is far more circumspect in his actions when faced with a target which can shoot back, and this additional worry may cause him to bungle his chances and allow the quarry to escape.

Similarly, the last few months have seen an expansion of the ECM aids available to Jaguars and Harriers, the former carrying jamming pods and Philips-Matra Phimat chaff/flare dispensers beneath the wings for the first time during a 'Red Flag' highly realistic training exercise from Nellis AFB, Nevada, early in 1983. Some Harriers received internal chaff/flare dispensers for the Falklands operation, and all now have provision for Sidewinders and are being modified with internal Marconi Zeus jamming equipment. Such apparatus provides the aircraft with protection against radar- and IR-guided missiles, greatly improving the prospects of a successful mission. Zeus will form part of an integrated radar warning and ECM suite for the Harrier GR3 and the future GR5, development of which began in 1983.

The South Atlantic war also saw Harriers fitted with a jamming apparatus rejoicing in the name of 'Blue Eric' — in effect, the basic Sky Shadow equipment of the Tornado repackaged in one of the Harrier's under-fuselage detachable cannon pods.

The considerable delay in supplying this equipment may seem unusual, but its origins lie in financial policies widespread not only in Britain, but generally throughout NATO. Officials in the USA have in the past commented unfavourably on their allies' habits of spending large sums on purchasing the best equipment available, and then finding that insufficient cash remains to obtain the necessary weapons — or in some extreme cases, fuel — to make an effective system. In the past few years, British government policy has been to reverse this trend by reducing expenditure in one area and devoting the saving to providing a complete range of offensive and defensive armament for a smaller number of systems. Thus the Harrier and Jaguar have gained at the expense of (for example) the Vulcan fleet and part of the Shackleton AEW2 force, both of which are being retired earlier than planned. The Falklands war again underlined the fact that ammunition usage in combat is invariably faster than allowed for in planning, with the result that fresh impetus has been given to an earlier-announced move to increase war stocks — including a doubling of the air-to-air missile inventory.

Strike Command's transport arm is an additional weapon in the hands of ground forces, enabling them to deploy rapidly with all save their heaviest equipment and receive regular

replenishment once in position. Hercules from the backbone of the air movements fleet, with helicopters moving supplies to the front line from dumps in the rearward areas. The twin-rotor Chinook HC1 with its 10-ton capacity has made a sizeable improvement possible in transport capability even though the lighter Puma is still a useful workhorse. Extensively equipped for operation at night and in most weathers (a new area for the tactical helicopter force) and fitted with radar warning receivers (RWR) to give indication of enemy presence, the Chinooks were previously assigned to deployments up to 100 miles behind the lines on account of their size and consequent vulnerability. Experience in the Falklands war has shown that this policy was perhaps over-cautious, and the procedure now is to move the Chinook base further forward, near the Puma detachments. Stress is nevertheless placed on rapid unloading and loading of the Chinook near to the scene of action (return journeys including casualty evacuation) and its ability to carry loads on three external hooks means that supplies can be provided to that number of troop positions in a single sortie without the need for landing.

Further Strike Command forces concentrate their attention on the sea threat, principally the submarine, for apart from carrying nuclear missiles these vessels would also wreak havoc on the trans-Atlantic shipping which would be an indispensable part of American support if NATO were attacked. An unceasing game of airborne cat and underwater mouse is played in the deep North Atlantic waters as Norwegian Orion maritime reconnaissance aircraft handover the submarines they have tracked leaving the major naval base at Murmansk, in the Soviet Arctic, to their NATO allies — the RAF's Nimrod MR2s included. Such vigilance is vital for the West in that it is an accurate thermometer of the Cold War: any sudden increase in submarine activity is an important indicator of Soviet intentions.

The ultimate destination of the data thus gained by the Nimrods on their long patrols is not revealed by the RAF, but it seems from other sources that it is shared amongst Britain's allies and provides useful intelligence for the US Navy's massive submarine tracking organisation. Barra sonobuoys dropped by the Nimrod MR2 transmit the acoustic signals received to AQS-901 processing equipment inside the aircraft, reportedly with such accuracy that the class of submarine can be determined by its sound signature alone.

The MR2's weapons fit provided for four Aérospatiale AS-12 anti-ship missiles under the wings and internal stores which included mines, depth charges and the new Stingray torpedo, but the Nimrod received additional capabilities as a result of the Falklands operation. Most noticeable was the refuelling probe for extended patrols, but the options of underwing Sidewinder defence weapons and internally-stowed Harpoon anti-ship missiles are now to be retained. It is stressed officially that the availability of these two missiles does not indicate a change of Nimrod tactics in regular North Atlantic operations (up till now the AS-12s had never been fitted), and attacks against surface vessels will remain the responsibility of the Buccaneer.

Since July 1983, the home-based Buccaneer S2 squadrons have been dedicated to maritime strike duties — a strange about-turn for an aircraft conceived to operate from an aircraft carrier aginst land targets. Based at Lossiemouth, Scotland, and assigned to SACLANT (NATO's Atlantic Command), the Buccaneer's main area of operation is the Iceland-Faroes gap, through which Soviet surface forces would pass on their way from Murmansk to the Atlantic. Armament in this role is the Martel missile (available in both anti-radar and TV-guided versions) and the laser-guided Pave Way bomb and its associated Pave Spike designator pod. Recently, new tactics have been operationally evaluated for Martel attack, when in March 1983, 10 Buccaneers deployed to a weapons range in Florida to practice low-level formation launches of the TV variant for the first time.

Allied Command Europe (ACE)

The Supreme Allied Commander, Europe (SACEUR) is responsible for the area from North Cape to the North African littoral and from the Atlantic to the eastern boundary of Turkey and for the Mediterranean and Baltic approaches. Headquarters are at SHAPE (Supreme Headquarters Allied Powers Europe), Casteau, Belgium. The post of SACEUR is always filled by a US officer who is also the national commander of US forces in Europe. SACEUR has British and German deputies. Forces are committed to SACEUR by all NATO countries except France and Iceland.

On 10 April 1975, RAF Strike Command was added to the NATO structure as United Kingdom Air Forces. Whereas only certain of its units were allocated to the Alliance prior to that date, all are now committed.

Allied Command Atlantic (ACLANT)

Allied Command Atlantic extends from the North Pole to the Tropic of Cancer and from the coastal waters of North America to those of Europe and Africa. The headquarters of the Supreme Allied Commander Atlantic are at Norfolk, Virginia. The post of SACLANT is always filled by a US Navy officer who is also the national commander of US Navy forces in the Atlantic. He has a British deputy. The countries committing forces to SACLANT are Canada, Denmark, the Netherlands, Portugal, the UK and USA. Belgium and Germany also contribute forces to STANAVFORLANT.

Allied Command Channel (ACCHAN)

ACCHAN extends from the Southern North Sea through the English Channel. The headquarters of Commander-in-Chief, Channel (CHINCHAN) who is always a British naval officer, are at Northwood, Middlesex. The Netherlands, and the UK commit forces to CHINCHAN, whilst Denmark, Germany and the US additionally provide forces for STANAVFORCHAN. A Channel Committee of the Naval Chiefs of Staff of Belgium, the Netherlands and the UK serves as an advisory and consultative body to CHINCHAN, who also holds the national appointment of C-in-C Fleet and the Major Subordinate Command of CINCEASTLANT.

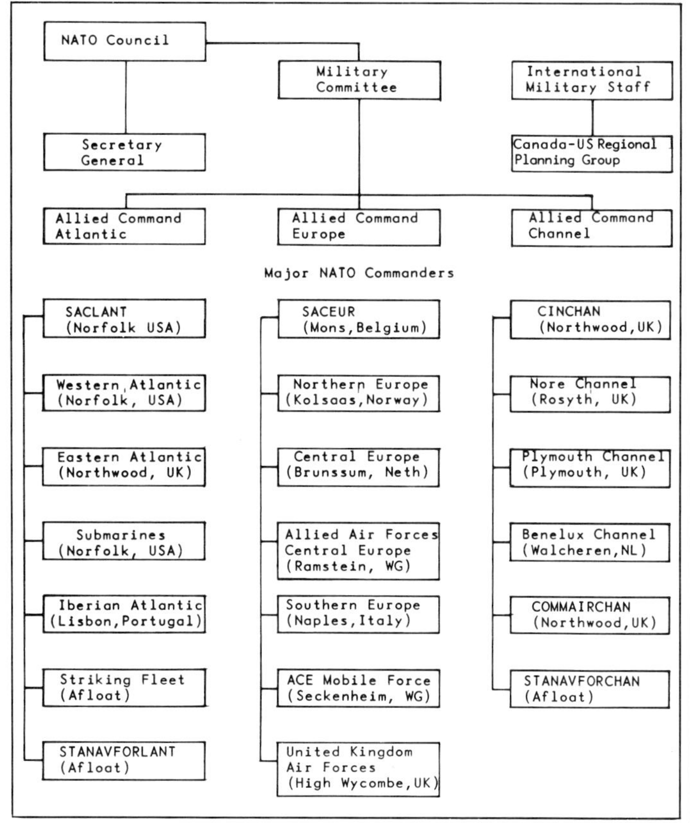

Abbreviations:

STANAVFORLANT — Standing Naval Force Atlantic
STANAVFORCHAN — Standing Naval Force Channel

RAF appointments:
AOC-in-C Strike Command is also C-in-C United Kingdom Air Forces (CINCUKAIR)
AOC No 18 Group is also Commander Maritime Air Eastern Atlantic (COMMAIREASTLANT) and Commander Maritime Air Channel (COMMAIRCHAN)

Note: Spain joined NATO in 1982, but the integration of its forces within the Alliance has yet to be finalised.

Tornado GR1s armed with the new Sea Eagle anti-ship missile were originally scheduled to supplant SACLANT's Buccaneers, but the priority allocation of these aircraft to RAF Germany has resulted in an extended lease of life for the Buccaneer until the 1990s. Sea Eagles will now equip Buccaneers in order to enhance their strike capabilities, the new system being more 'clever' than its carrier aircraft. With the Buccaneer's avionics as they now stand, the value of Sea Eagle is largely nullified by the fact that the aircraft must approach to within Martel-type range before it can identify its target and release the weapon. This shortcoming is to be rectified by improvements to the Buccaneer's nav/attack systems, from 1986 onwards, whilst jamming equipment will be improved and chaff dispensers fitted.

Mention of maritime operations by Strike Command would not be complete without reference to the SAR flights of Wessex HC2s and Sea King HAR3s located around Britain's shores, interlinked on the South Coast and Western Scotland by units of the Royal Navy. In an average year, the RAF's rescue helicopters are called out on about 900 occasions — over land as well as water — and save some 700 civilian and military lives.

Defence against foul weather and bad fortune is but a minor activity compared with the effort expended on protection of 55

Above:
Based at Leuchars, just across the Firth of Tay from Dundee, No 111 Squadron operates Phantom FGR1s. The new light grey camouflage scheme and small, pale roundels are compromised by decorative unit markings on the nose and fin, but would be removed in time of conflict. *MoD*

million lives from air attack. This daunting responsibility is entrusted to Strike Command's interceptor force, currently comprising five squadrons of Phantoms (one of which is deployed to the Falkland Islands) and two of Lightings, but before these can engage the enemy, information must be gathered on his position and course. This is the responsibility of three Sector Operations Centres at Buchan, Boulmer and Neatished which process information from nine UK Air Defence Ground Environment (UKADGE) radar stations and several other sources including NATO radar posts on the Continent. As part of a 10-year modernisation programme for air defence begun in 1977, one-quarter of all RAF equipment funds its being expended in this area, with NATO meeting most of the cost of updating the UKADGE stations through the addition of new three-dimensional L- and S-band radars, display and communications equipment. The process will also allow the duties of a damaged control centre to be shouldered by its neighbour — something not previously possible in full — and will include new mobile radar units.

The lesson that surface-based radars are unable to detect low-flying aircraft until it is too late was painfully driven home in the Falklands war, although in this case the omission was one of providing a carrier-based AEW (airborne early warning) system. However, home defences have included the Shackleton AEW2 and its 1940s technology AN/APS-20 airborne search radar since 1972, and a vastly superior aircraft is now becoming available in the form of the Nimrod AEW3 conversion of the maritime patroller. With its GEC-Marconi Mission System Avionics, including scanners in grotesquely-bulged nose and tail fairings, the Nimrod AEW3 has been produced specifically to RAF requirements for a primary over-water role, its six-man tactical team having the ability to direct friendly fighters on to incoming air threats as well as simultaneously plotting surface ships for the benefit of strike forces.

Below:
On the eve of its retirement, a Shackleton AEW2 is saluted by its replacement, the Nimrod AEW3. Although both aircraft were built at Woodford, they will operate from different bases, Nimrods being stationed at Waddington, whilst the Shackletons were at Lossiemouth with No 8 Squadron. Of note are the Wing Commander's pennant and the squadron's Arabian dagger emblem on the nose, and the yellow/blue/red bars flanking the roundel — the only such example of a four-engined aircraft carrying the last-mentioned markings. *BAe*

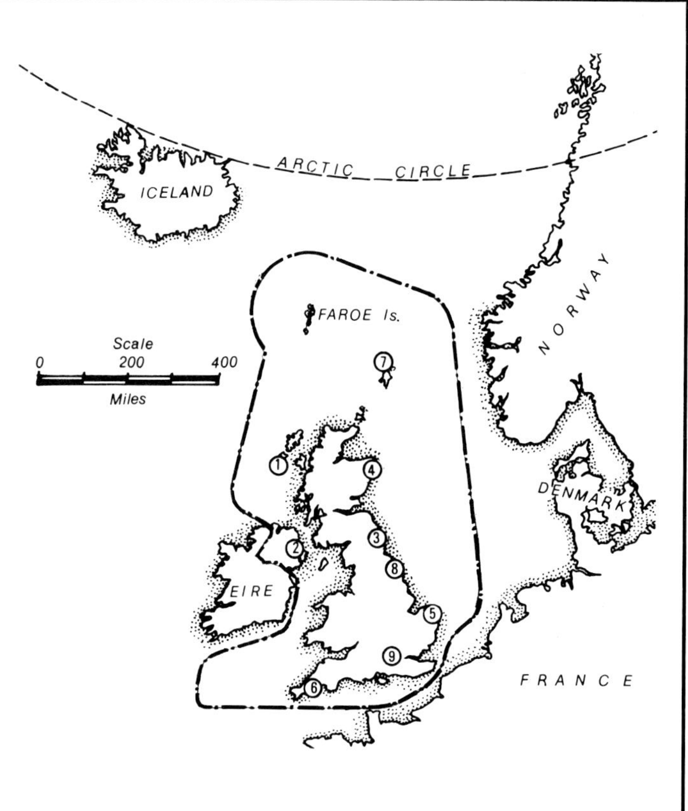

UKADR radar/control sites

1	Benbecula	The UKADR forms part of NATO
2	Bishops Court	Early Warning Area 12, and in
3	Boulmer	the Alliance context, CINCUKAIR
4	Buchan	(AOC-in-C Strike Command) is
5	Neatished	Regional Air Defence Commander
6	Portreath	for the UK area. Day-to-day
7	Saxa Vord	operational control is delegated
8	Staxton Wold	by CINCUKAIR to the AOC of No 11
9	West Drayton	Group, however.

Sharing its information with the similar NATO force of Boeing E-3A Sentries — an agreement for pooling data having been signed in 1982 — the Nimrod will undertake patrols of up to seven hours' duration as far as 1,000 miles from its base at Waddington. This will allow significant changes to be effected in the present air defence policy, in that low-flying aircraft can be intercepted at much greater distances from their intended targets than is now the case.

Accompanying the Nimrod AEW3 on its long-range patrols later this decade will be the Tornado F2 variant of the GR1 interdictor/strike aircraft. Unique to the RAF (although some interest has been evinced abroad), the F2 features Foxhunter intercept radar and additional fuel in a lengthened fuselage to overcome the traditional deficiency of British-produced fighters: short legs. With two external fuel tanks it can loiter for some two hours at 450 miles from home with reserves for 10 minutes of combat, and a retracting refuelling probe allows much longer sorties to be accomplished when a tanker aircraft is available. Working in conjunction with a Nimrod AEW3 the Tornado fighter will provide Strike Command with the means to strengthen its defences to the west — a particularly vital area now that Soviet long-range interdictors such as the Tu-22 'Blinder' have the ability to penetrate from this direction after a flight down the Atlantic from their Arctic bases.

Until the first operational Tornado F2 squadron is formed in late-1986, Lightnings and Phantoms will continue as the prime Strike Command interceptors from their East Coast bases at Leuchars, Binbrook, Coningsby and Wattisham. In peacetime, the interceptor units are far from idle, for in addition to regular training exercises they are called upon to investigate unidentified aircraft penetrating the UK Air Defence Region which is part of NATO Early Warning Area 12. Personnel take turns to undertake the lonely vigil of Quick Reaction Alert (QRA) at each base, whiling away the time in a purpose-built hangar containing two fighters fully armed and ready to go, until they are scrambled to intercept an unknown target. On an average of five times per week this will prove to be a Soviet aircraft on Atlantic patrol or an electronic intelligence-gathering snooper sent to monitor procedures and frequencies, and these will be escorted until leaving the area. No action is taken to head-off interlopers as long as they keep to free airspace, and it is notable in this connection that the Lightning F6 was retrospectively fitted with cannon armament in order that it can give a warning 'shot across the bows' to an intruder rather than being restricted to missiles as the only course of action.

A new departure in the air defence organisation is the arming of Hawk T1s with all-aspect AIM-9L Sidewinders. These missiles proved highly effective during the Falklands campaign when Sea Harriers destroyed 16 Argentine aircraft

Below:
Crewing-up for a training sortie is a Phantom FGR2 of No 29 Squadron at Coningsby wearing the light grey camouflage to which all interceptors are gradually converting. *P. A. Jackson*

Bottom:
Lightning colours are in the process of change from upper surface green/grey camouflage to two-tone grey overall, although experiments have been made with different shades, to find the best combination. As demonstrated by these two Lightning F6s, a much darker top has been introduced recently, modelled by aircraft 'BJ' of No 11 Squadron. Note that 'DF' of the Lightning Training Flight lacks the retrospective installation of a cannon pack in the forward portion of the belly fuel tank.
P. A. Jackson

without loss to themselves, although their value will be diminished when carried by aircraft not equipped with radar. A stand-by force of 72 Hawk 'interceptors' will be provided by giving Sidewinder provision to 95 aircraft used in the advanced weapons-training role and by the Red Arrows aerobatic team, the former being flown by instructors. A non-radar aircraft armed with short-range infra-red homing missiles must achieve visual contact before releasing its weapon, and thus demands considerable assistance from ground control. It may be recalled that in the 1982 air battles between Israel and Syria involved close-in fighting by radar-equipped aircraft which could, in theory, have joined battle from afar, though it is wise to bear in mind that the weather at low altitude over Britain is seldom as clear as conditions in the Middle East.

Completing the air defence force are the SAM batteries: Bloodhound 2 and Rapier. The former is now an obsolescent system used in the low and medium levels rather than the high altitudes for which it was designed, the absence of a successor — eventually to be produced, it is hoped, by a European consortium — requiring a further round of improvements to be incorporated shortly. Anticipating that the bulk of interdiction sorties against Britain would be made via the shortest route, Strike Command had deployed its Bloodhounds along England's East Coast where the three flights of SAMs have recently been augmented by a similar number brought back from RAF Germany. The point-defence Rapier — another star performer in the South Atlantic — is operated by the RAF Regiment to protect the Scottish airfields at Leuchars and Lossiemouth, the same unit also being responsible for manning the Rapiers bought by the United State for defence of USAF bases in Britain.

As noted above, airborne refuelling is a central element in the RAF's daily operations and one which is in the process of considerable expansion. It is now 25 years since converted Valiant bombers began the first refuelling service for RAF combat aircraft, and when this type was prematurely withdrawn with metal fatigue the task was assigned to Victors, also re-mustered from the nuclear role. Apart from keeping interceptors tanked-up during their escort missions for Soviet intelligence-gathering aircraft, Victors are responsible for backing-up overseas deployments of aircraft. Normally, this is for a training mission such as a weapons camp in Cyprus or a 'Red Flag' exercise in the USA, but the Victor force took on sterner tasks when it was heavily committed to the Falklands war operations.

Whilst able to carry its own empty weight in fuel, the Victor is a small tanker by today's standards, as evidenced by the fact that 11 aircraft had to make 15 sorties to refuel single Vulcans for each of the 7,500-mile round trips from Ascension Island to the Falklands (see diagram in Chapter 5). Though six Hercules and a similar number of Vulcans were hastily converted to tankers in the wake of the Falklands conflict, longer-term plans call for a fleet of VC10s to assume the airborne refuelling role, the first of which are now being delivered. The VC10 K2 and Super VC10 K3 represent a change in refuelling aircraft policy in that they will not only be able to refuel fighters deploying overseas, but also carry associated equipment and personnel for the first time, thereby reducing the need for accompanying transports.

This theme has been taken one stage further in the purchase of six TriStar 500s for refuelling conversion, a move made as the result of additional commitments assumed for maintaining

Above:
Six flights of Bloodhound 2 SAMs augment the RAF's manned interceptors at bases along England's east coast. As yet, no firm replacement plans have been announced for this ageing weapon. *RAF Official*

Above right:
Hawks are now being equipped with AIM-9L Sidewinders for point-defence duties in an emergency. Appropriate modifications will be embodied in 95 aircraft in order to provide a force of 72 to be declared to NATO. *BAe*

Right:
Short range air defence at Lossiemouth and Leuchars airfields in Scotland is provided by Rapier SAMs of the RAF Regiment. Rapiers were credited with the destruction of 14 Argentine aircraft (plus six probables) during the Falklands war. *BAe*

Top:
Most of the standard–length Hercules C1s in Strike Command are now equipped with in-flight refuelling probes. The installation was first tried-out in XV200 on 3 May 1982, using a Victor K2 tanker of No 57 Squadron. *MoD*

Above:
A few Harrier trainers operated by No 233 OCU at Wittering lack the nose-mounted laser ranger and are known as T Mk 4As. Occupying the rear seat of this aircraft is HRH Prince Charles, who visited Wittering in July 1977. *RAF Official*

Below:
Tornado GR1s may be fitted with a 'bolt-on' flight-refuelling probe which is stowed along the fuselage side when not in use. *P. A. Jackson*

Below right:
A radar screen under jamming attack by Canberra T17s of No 360 Squadron, the three parallel lines at the lower left being generated by chaff ('Window') and the remaining disturbance by electronic means. Radar operators must be able to direct interceptions under these seemingly impossible conditions. *P. A. Jackson*

the Falklands garrison. Approximately similar in performance to the KC-10A Extenders now being supplied to the USAF, the TriStar can do the work of three VC10s or nine Victors in certain situations, or haul the equivalent in mixed freight of four or five Hercules and still carry a substantial fuel load. The South Atlantic war has also been responsible for some RAF aircraft sprouting receiver probes: in addition to the already equipped Buccaneer, Lightning, Phantom, Harrier, Tornado and Jaguar aircraft, inflight refuelling capability has been extended to the Nimrod MR2, AEW3 and Hercules. The latter is considered to have sufficient unrefuelled range for all possible tasks (the record time in air for a Hercules is over 24 hours!), but will continue to carry the probes fitted for their Falklands role — just in case.

Maintenance of Strike Command forces in peak condition is a never-ending process involving Operational Conversion Units (OCU) and specialist squadrons. Having learnt to fly with Support Command, newly qualified personnel intended for the 'sharp end' of the RAF transfer to Strike Command for

specialist instruction. Those destined for single- or two-seat combat types will attend the Tactical Weapons Units (TWU) where Hawks provide them with experience of working with armament. As stressed earlier, low flying skills are an essential prerequisite in the business of remaining undetected in a hostile environment, and training at the TWU therefore involves polishing-up the experience already gained with a Flying Training School (FTS).

OCUs in the Command mostly specialise in a single aircraft type and bridge the gap between TWU and an operational squadron; transport, tanker and helicopter personnel omit the TWU stage and reach OCU fresh from an FTS. The 'Operational' side of the OCU is taken seriously, some units having the 'shadow' identity of an RAF squadron which would be adopted in time of war. Those which do not are assigned to reinforce other squadrons or undertake supporting roles, ensuring that no aircraft are left idle when the RAF is mobilised.

Other proficiency tasks are largely the responsibility of the dwindling fleet of Canberras, their function generally being to provide a wide range of targets for air defence units. Canberras tow banner and sleeve targets for interceptor aircraft and the Navy's gunners respectively; solid, missile-shaped targets for Rapier SAM units; and undertake mock attacks on the latter for training. They also take part in 'raids' on Britain to test fighter control techniques.

Soviet policy of including in each air operation force some 30% electronic jamming aircraft emphasises the need for radar operators — in aircraft as well as on the ground — to be able to work in the face of intensive jamming. The bulbous-nosed Canberra T17 with its array of disruptive electronics, as well as old-fashioned, but still very effective chaff ('Window'), is the main weapon in this regularly rehearsed war scenario. The T17s are accompanied in their raids by 'silent' Canberras which transmit no electromagnetic signals and attempt to slip-in unnoticed whilst the jammers distract the defence. The black art of electronic warfare is constantly changing, and the RAF must be aware of all new developments in order to remain effective in attack and defence.

Considerable emphasis has been placed on developing techniques of battle-damage repair (BDR) in recent years, and this proved to have been time well spent when aircraft suffered small-arms fire in the Falklands. A lucky hit with even a rifle bullet can ground a vital combat aircraft for days until spares arrive (if they do at all in the heat of battle) and the timely study of ways to keep aircraft flying under such circumstances has given Britain a clear lead over most air arms in BDR procedures.

Small external holes are covered with adhesive aluminium tape, and metal sheets are riveted over larger areas, whilst internal damage is patched-up with roughly-manufactured replacements, except in cases where the aircraft has been structurally weakened to an unsafe extent. Fresh techniques and improvisations continue to appear, and it is no exaggeration to say that BDR will have a significant effect on the number of aircraft available for operations on the second and subsequent mornings of a battle.

Mention has already been made of some aircraft modifications embodied during or as a result of the Falklands war, and analysis of its experiences in that conflict has given Strike Command a rare opportunity to conduct a wide-ranging reappraisal of equipment and tactics and their future application. Though unprepared (as a result of Government policy, and through no fault of its own) for such a long-distance

operation, the RAF overcame the myriad difficulties associated with moving men and equipment into battle and rapidly adapted its aircraft to operate with new weapons and avionics. Some of the requirements were already obvious before the Falklands war, but could only be met when the necessary finance was at last released. Others were in the development or planning stage and will now be accelerated.

The Vulcan raids on Port Stanley airfield gained limited success and underlined the need for the JP233 area-denial weapons dispenser now being produced for the Tornado GR1. Attacks by the Vulcans with Shrike missiles on radar sites were also not completely successful and a new anti-radar missile is to be procured for the Tornado force as a matter of priority. The 'vital' fitment of chaff/flare dispensers and jamming pods to Harriers has resulted in further applications to the Jaguar force, and all Harriers are now also equipped to carry Sidewinders, with Jaguars no doubt to follow. Plans have been accelerated for installation of chaff/flare equipment and active jammers in all front-line aircraft.

Forward air control procedures are being re-examined in the light of experience, with particular emphasis on laser designation and improvement of ground-air communications, whilst tactical reconnaissance facilities (in the absence of Jaguars to support the Task Force) were found inadequate and are to be augmented. Transport and tanker aircraft were given navigation systems to provide the means for accuracy when making a long-range refuelling rendezvous during the conflict, and this capability will be retained.

Taken in total, these small modifications amount to a change of policy for Strike Command. With the exception of a few overseas deployments, the RAF has concentrated its efforts during the past decade into providing an efficient fighting force for NATO, covering the home base, Germany and the North Atlantic. Now, however, it is charged with reinforcement of the Falklands in an emergency, and its aircraft and personnel must be able to change from one role to the other at short notice. New equipment for the maintenance of

the Falklands garrison has been selected with NATO commitments in mind, and can meet both requirements.

This new-found long-range reinforcement role does not herald a return to the global strategy which ended in the early-1970s when British forces withdrew from the Middle and Far East, for the needs of NATO will continue to be the prime task of Strike Command. The Falklands war of 1982 was a diversion from the principal commitment, but a valuable exercise in that it proved beyond doubt that the RAF was capable of undertaking its assigned roles and adaptable enough to convert rapidly to others. Performance has been improved from experience, and Britain and NATO are more secure as a result.

Above:
. . . and the propeller-powered Rushton Winch Pack beneath the TT18's wing can stream a drogue or, as in this case, a missile-shaped target, on up to 9½ miles of cable. The latter, normally towed 3¾ miles behind the aircraft, is fitted with a cluster of six flares on its fin to aid acquisition by SAMs. *P. A. Jackson*

Below:
Two Hunting JP233 airfield attack weapons can be carried beneath the fuselage of the Tornado GR1. Each pod is in two parts, the forward component housing HB876 area-denial mines, and the rear element, SG357 cratering munitions. Both are simultaneously ejected over the target, the container remaining with the aircraft. *BAe*

3. ORGANISATION

The process of RAF contraction, whereby former operational commands were reduced to group status within an all-embracing Strike Command, has continued to the present day with consequent changes in organisation and responsibilities. Most recently, in November 1983, this has involved the merging of what were in former times Bomber and Transport Commands into a new group with wide-ranging tasks, leaving Strike Command with just three major components.

Administration of Strike Command is ultimately vested in the government of the day. Government policy decides the roles to be undertaken and the financial resources devoted to defence, and in consultation with the Joint Chiefs of Staff Committee, priorities are determined and cash allocations made to the three Services. From time to time, conflicts arise between the tasks allocated and the finance provided for their execution, and to resolve such differences the Chiefs of Staff have the right of joint access to the Prime Minister. In theory, the heads of each Service select the equipment needed for their roles, but the high cost of modern weapons and the political ramifications of allocating valuable contracts have resulted in the government influencing purchasing policy.

The RAF's chain of command begins with the Ministry of Defence (Air) in the person of the Chief of Air Staff. From MoD headquarters in Whitehall, London, executive orders are passed to Strike Command HQ at Naphill near High Wycombe, Support Command and RAF Germany. In the first case, the chain continues to three groups (Nos 1, 11 and 18) and ultimately to their component squadrons. Where several squadrons at a station are tasked with a similar role, base operations is responsible for assignment of duties to the individual unit.

Following an efficiency and cost-saving study, the decision was announced in 1982 to merge Nos 1 and 38 Groups during the next year. Previously No 1 Group had comprised Tornados, Buccaneers, Vulcans, Victor tankers and the Canberra force, whilst No 38 was the RAF's Mobility Group, combining transports and fighter-bomber squadrons. For traditional reasons, the amalgamated group is known as No 1, although the Buccaneers and Canberras have been transferred elsewhere (and Vulcan B2s retired). No 38 Group disbanded on 18 November 1983 and No 1 Group HQ moved from Bawtry to the No 38 Group base at Upavon. In effect, therefore, the new No 1 Group is basically No 38 with the addition of Tornados and Victors.

Below:

Tornado IDS variants of all three operator nations are based at the Trinational Tornado Training Establishment, Cottesmore, where pilots and navigators are converted to the aircraft before receiving weapons training in their own countries. The code combination 'B-12' identifies this aircraft as British.

STRIKE COMMAND ORGANISATION

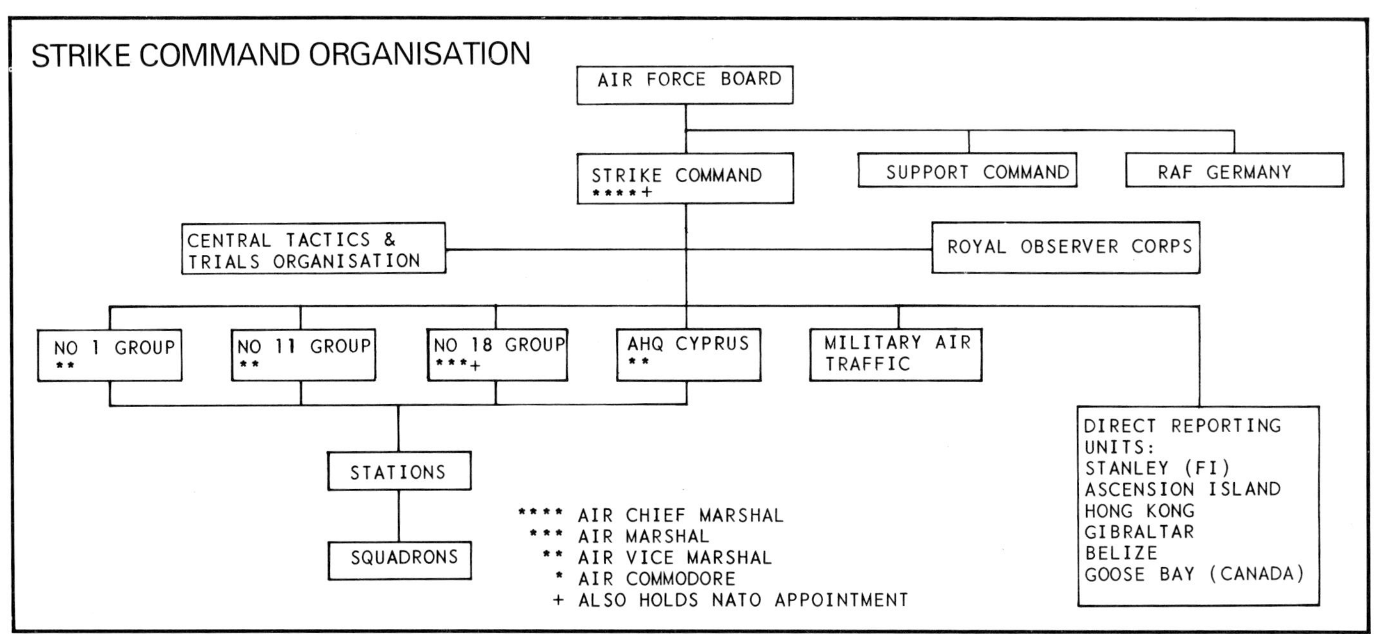

STRIKE COMMAND OPERATING BASES: Key

A High Wycombe
B Northwood
C Stanmore
D Upavon
1 Aldergrove
2 Barkston Heath
3 Bawdsey
4 Benson
5 Binbrook
6 Boulmer
7 Brawdy
8 Brize Norton
9 Chivenor
10 Coltishall
11 Conningsby
12 Cottesmore
13 Finningley
14 Honington
15 Kinloss
16 Leconfield
17 Leuchars
18 Lossiemouth
19 Lyneham
20 Manston
21 Marham
22 North Coates
23 Northolt
24 Odiham
25 St Mawgan
26 Turnhouse
27 Valley
28 Waddington
29 Wattisham
30 West Raynham
31 Wittering
32 Wyton

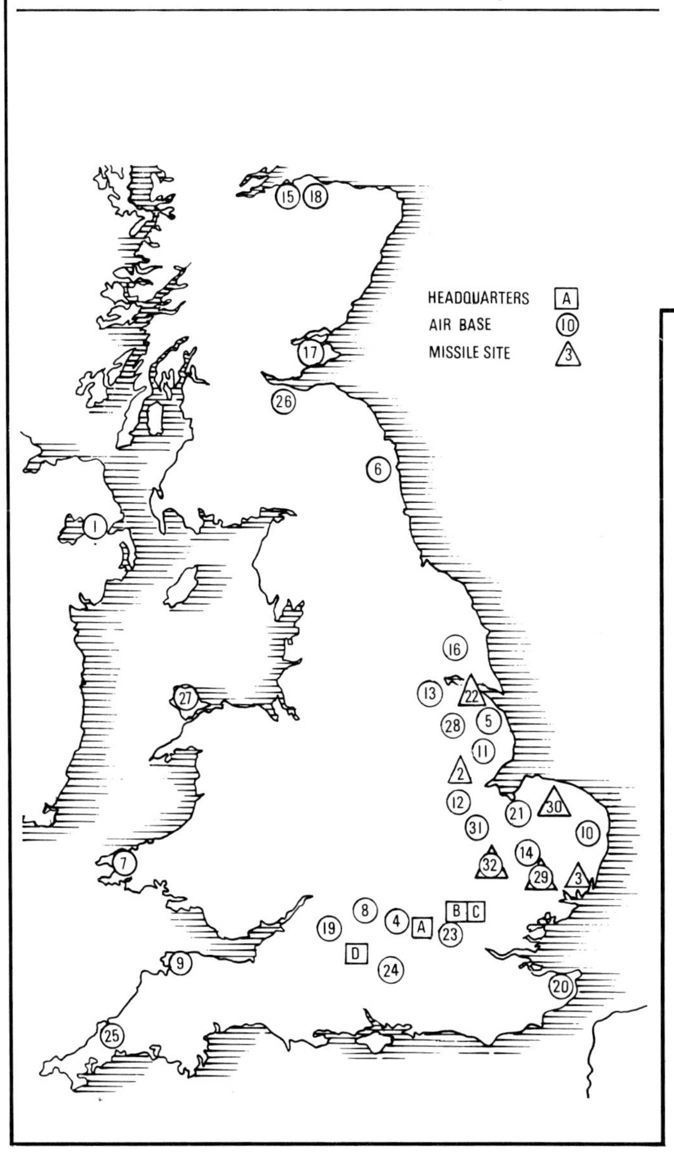

No 1 Group, Crest.

Above:
No 57 Squadron, representing one half of the Strike Command force of 22 Victor K2s, replaced its former '57' fin logo with the official badge of a blue Phoenix rising from red flames during 1982. Here, one of the unit's aircraft gives a Nimrod MR2 the opportunity to try–out its newly–acquired probe. *BAe*

Right:
A major boost for the aerial refuelling fleet is now coming on line with deliveries of VC10 K2 and K3 tankers to No 101 Squadron at Brize Norton. Prototype conversion ZA141 wears green/grey upper surface camouflage, but all others have been finished with a hemp top. *BAe*

No 1 Group

No 1 Group has now achieved its authorised strength of three Tornado squadrons, a conversion establishment and a weapons unit, and present deliveries of the type are being made to RAF Germany, the initial squadrons having been formed in Britain. At Cottesmore, the Tri-national Tornado Training Establishment is charged with converting pilots and navigators of all four air arms operating the aircraft (RAF, Italian AF, German AF and German Navy) and has a strength of 50 Tornados including 21 RAF models, the first of which arrived in July 1980 prior to the start of the initial conversion course on 5 January 1982. Weapons training is the responsibility of individual countries, RAF crews progressing to Honington's Tornado Weapons Conversion Unit before a squadron posting. Sharing Honington is No 9 Squadron, the first operational Tornado unit, formed on 1 June 1982, whilst Marham houses Nos 617 and 27 Squadrons, established during 1983.

The Victor K2 tanker fleet of 22 aircraft is also based at Marham in conjunction with No 232 OCU which borrows aircraft from resident Nos 55 and 57 Squadrons on an 'as required' basis. VC10 tanker-transports comprise five K2s and four Super VC10 K3s obtained from civilian airlines and converted by BAe at Filton to the new configuration, although 11 more ex-British Airways Supers are held in storage at Abingdon for eventual replacement of the ageing Victors. Tanker VC10s of No 101 Squadron, formed officially in April 1984, are deployed at Brize Norton alongside the transport versions delivered to No 10 Squadron from 1966 onwards and the two BAe146 C1s supplied in 1983 for operational trials. Brize is also the base of No 241 OCU in the large jet transport conversion role and of six TriStar 500 tanker-transports bought from British Airways early in 1983 and converted by Marshall of Cambridge. Four will later be fitted with large

cargo doors and reinforced floors to expand their transport capabilities. The refuelling Vulcan K2s — six aircraft of No 50 Squadron at Waddington — have been phased-out with the arrival of VC10 K2s and K3s from conversion, their adoption for this role being a stop-gap measure between the Falklands war and the previously-planned development of the tanker fleet.

No 1 Group's responsibilities include provision of forces for two rapid deployment units, the UK Mobile Force and NATO's Allied Command Europe Mobile Force (UKMF and AMF), plus strike aircraft to be used under the control and the NATO Supreme Allied Commander Europe (SACEUR). The AMF — popularly termed the 'NATO Fire Brigade' — comprises land and air elements from all member countries which are dispatched to a point of tension to underline to a potential aggressor the Alliance's dictum that an attack upon one is upon all. A national role is reserved for the UKMF, but it can be placed at the disposal of NATO if required.

Heading these forces are the Jaguar GR1s and Harrier GR3s based at Coltishall and Wittering respectively. There are three Jaguar squadrons — Nos 6 and 54 in the close air support and strike role, with No 41 being divided equally between tactical reconnaissance and ground attack with cluster-bombs. Their conversion unit is No 226 OCU at Lossiemouth. No 1 Squadron flies Harriers for close air support and battlefield interdiction, the aircraft's single left-facing camera providing a limited day reconnaissance facility. No 233 OCU is also at Wittering for Harrier conversion, and

Top:
Strike Command's transport and tanker capability is being considerably improved during 1984 with delivery of six former British Airways TriStar 500s. The first aircraft to be painted in RAF colours is seen here at Cambridge in July 1983 prior to conversion. *Marshal of Cambridge*

Above:
Six Vulcans were hurriedly converted to K Mk 2 tankers during the Falklands war, but entered service too late for operational use. The lead aircraft of this pair is refuelling a standard B Mk 2 retained for conversion training.

Right:
Closeup of the refuelling hose drum unit. *P. A. Jackson*

it is expected that a second operational unit will form there in 1987 with Harrier GR3s withdrawn from RAF Germany with the advent of the Harrier GR5. No OCUs are operated by the RAF on the Continent, and thus No 1 Group units train personnel for Germany.

Like the Jaguar and Harrier squadrons, No 1 Group's helicopters are prepared to move base at a moment's notice, usually to a location literally 'in the field' where aircrew, technicians and communications personnel will live in tented accommodation. Odiham is the base of the tactical helicopter force, housing the Chinook HC1s of No 7 Squadron, Puma HC1s of No 33 Squadron, and No 240 OCU with both types. The RAF received 33 Chinooks and 47 Pumas, although eight more of the former have been ordered for delivery from 1984 to augment the force and replace three lost on *Atlantic Conveyor* in the Falklands war.

Tactical transport facilities are provided by the Lyneham Transport Wing, comprising 61 Hercules of Nos 24, 30, 47 and 70 Squadrons and No 242 OCU. These fly an average of 10 million air miles each year, and to increase their bulk cargo capacity, 30 have been converted to Hercules C3 standard with an additional 15ft of cargo hold length in a programme just drawing to a close. Most remaining C1s have become C1Ps with an in-flight refuelling probe above the cockpit, and in the wake of the Falklands war, six became C(K)1s with a refuelling hose drum unit mounted on the rear cargo ramp. They principally operate from Port Stanley to support aircraft making the Falkland Islands run.

Leading the lighter transport units is The Queen's Flight at Benson, flying three Andover CC2s and two Wessex HCC4s. These carry members of the Royal Family, senior Government ministers and Chiefs of Staff on their official duties, plus visit-

Left:

Training exercises are accompanied by few of the luxuries of life on an air base. Tucked into the side of a wood in Denmark and covered by camouflage netting are the two communications trucks constituting the 'operations room' of the AMF Helicopter Unit during exercise 'Amber Express' in September 1981.
P. A. Jackson

Below:

Here a Puma of No 33 Squadron lifts a 105mm light gun during the AMF Exercise 'Hardfall'. *MoD*

Bottom:

Chinook HC1s of the Odiham battlefield helicopter force demonstrate their versatility in carrying armoured vehicles and troops. During the Falklands war, a Chinook transported 81 fully-equipped soldiers — almost twice its normal complement of 44.
RAF Official

Top:
A typical tactical situation for the Hercules short-field landing and take off. Here a No 47 Squadron aircraft is seen at Pope AFB. *RAF Official*

Top right:
Three Andover CC2s serve in the distinctive colours of the Queen's Flight at Benson — white fuselage, red flying surfaces and a blue cheat line. They are expected to be replaced by two BAe 146 srs 100s in 1985. *BAe*

Above:
The RAF has expanded its fleet of BAe 125s so that the ageing Devons and Pembrokes can be retired. New 125s are the fan-engined Series 700 variety, although six earlier aircraft have been similarly re-engined for economic and environmental reasons.
P. A. Jackson

Right:
The Queen's Flight at Benson operates two Wessex HCC4s which are in constant use for VVIP flights. As yet, no successor has been nominated for replacement. *Westland*

ing heads of state. Replacement of the Andovers is in prospect by two new BAe146s if the trial operation by a pair of 100 Series aircraft proves satisfactory. Remaining transports operate from Northolt, where No 207 Squadron has 12 aged Devons and No 32 operates three Andover C2s, a cranked-fuselage Andover C1, 10 HS125s and two Gazelle HCC4s. It was originally proposed that Devons be replaced by 14 Beech Super King Airs or BAe Jetstream 31s, but this plan has been abandoned in favour of increasing the 125 fleet from its original six.

Four HS125 CC3s with Garrett turbofan engines were delivered early in 1983, and at the same time the six Viper-powered CC1s and CC2s returned to BAe to be brought up to the new standard. Two more 125 purchases were made at the same time to permit replacement of Devons and the six Pembrokes assigned to RAF Germany. Two special versions of the Andover, the E3 and E3A are operated by No 115 Squadron from Benson for calibration of navigation aids at RAF bases, these variants being easily distinguished by liberal application of red paint and, in the case of the E3, a spotlight in the nose to aid acquisition by theodolite operators on the ground. Crew conversion for all Andovers is provided by the Andover Training Flight, which separated from No 241 OCU in January 1983 when it joined No 115 Squadron in a move from Brize Norton.

Above:

Two BAe 146-100s were ordered for the RAF in 1982 and entered service with No 241 OCU at Brize Norton in the following year. Assigned to general transport duties, they are also being assessed for suitability for The Queen's Flight. The RAF designation is BAe 146 C1. *BAe*

Below:

Although bearing all the outward signs of being an Andover E3 of No 115 Squadron, XS644 is the unique Andover C1(Mod) testbed of the Wyton-based Electronic Warfare Avionics Unit. *P. A. Jackson*

No 11 Group

From headquarters at Bentley Priory, Stanmore, North London, No 11 Group administers Strike Command's air defence force of aircraft, SAMs and radar units. Providing airborne early warning are the six Shackleton AEW2s of No 8 Squadron operating from Lossiemouth, the force having been halved in 1981 as an economy measure. Replacement is now beginning with the far more capable Nimrod AEW3, 11 of which are being converted from MR1s and will be based at Waddington.

The oldest fighter in the group is the BAC Lightning F6, equipping Nos 5 and 11 Squadrons at Binbrook. Each unit has a small number of F3 variants, whilst the Lightning Training Flight and Lightning Augmentation Flight use both types, plus the two-seat T5 trainer. Some 70 Lightnings are based at Binbrook including a substantial reserve, yet plans have been abandoned for formation of a third squadron and the LTF has instead been given a 'shadow' operational role by way of partial compensation. All other interceptors are Phantoms, comprising ex-Navy FG1s of Nos 43 and 111 Squadrons at Leuchars and FGR2s at Coningsby (No 29 Squadron and No 228 OCU) and Wattisham (No 56 Squadron). No 29 Squadron deployed to Stanley in the Falkland Islands in October 1982 and was relieved by No 23 Squadron from Wattisham in April 1983. In order to keep home strength to its normal levels with the absence of one squadron in the South Atlantic, 15 ex-US Marine Corps F-4J Phantoms (powered by J79 engines instead of the RR Spey used in the FG1 and FGR2) have been bought to equip a further squadron of Strike Command. In the longer term, Tornado F2s will be issued to No 11 Group, beginning in 1985 with No 228 OCU, and continuing after 18 months to the Lightning squadrons, then the Phantom units, although four of the latter will be retained for as long as possible. Two squadrons of Tornados will each be based at Leuchars and Wattisham, and Leeming will become the home of a further three.

Also under the control of No 11 Group are No 1 Tactical Weapons Unit at Brawdy and No 2 TWU at Chivenor, each operating camouflaged Hawk T1s; No 1 TWU also has a diminishing number of Hunters and a few Jet Provost T4s (also camouflaged) for training forward air controllers. RAF orders for the Hawk totalled 175 (an option on a further 18 was not taken up) and these are shared with No 4 FTS and the Central Flying School of Support Command, the latter being the parent unit of the famous Red Arrows. TWU aircraft are adorned with the insignia of their shadow units, No 1 TWU comprising Nos 79 and 234 Squadrons, whilst No 2 TWU is otherwise Nos 63 and 151 Squadrons.

Above:
No 11 Group crest.

Below:
Parked outside Binbrook's control tower, the Lightning T5 is a two-seat trainer version of the F Mk 3 interceptor. It retains full operational capacity, as evidenced by the in-flight refuelling probe and two Red Top missiles. *P. A. Jackson*

Above right:
Overflying the Welsh coast, a Hunter FGA9 displays No 79 Squadron markings, indicating its attachment to No 1 TWU at Brawdy. A few Hunters supplement Hawks in the weapons-training role.

Right:
A spectacular sheet of flame belches from the rocket pod of a No 234 Squadron/No 1 TWU Hawk T1 as it releases its weapons at a training target. *BAe*

No 18 Group

Maritime tasks are the function of No 18 Group with its headquarters at Northwood, Middlesex, where the AOC holds the NATO appointments of Commander Maritime Air Eastern Atlantic and Commander Maritime Air Channel. The group recently gained a dedicated strike force of Buccaneer S2Bs when Nos 12 and 208 Squadrons transferred from the old No 1 Group. These squadrons are now based at Lossiemouth and assigned to SACLANT for anti-shipping duties with Martel missiles and 1,000lb bombs, principally in the Iceland-Faroes gap and Western Approaches. Following the Buccaneer fatigue problems in 1980, the aircraft from No 216 Squadron were absorbed and No 12 included an element equipped with Pave Spike designators and Pave Way laser-guided bombs — the former No 216 role. No 208, originally an over-land strike squadron, moved to Lossiemouth from Honington in July 1983 to adopt the anti-shipping role and was joined by No 237 OCU which flies some non-Martel Buccaneer S2As and Hunter trainers equipped with some of the former's systems (there being no dual-control Buccaneer). OCU Buccaneers have an operational role as tankers, refuelling their companions and Tornados with a 'Buddy Pack' beneath the starboard wing.

Ocean surveillance is assigned to four Nimrod squadrons, of which three (Nos 120, 201 and 206) constitute the Kinloss Wing. This Scottish base received the first of 35 MR2s (converted from MR2s by BAe at Woodford) in August 1979, and the programme is due for completion in mid-1984 when No 42 Squadron at St Mawgan will have received its full complement of updated aircraft. Training is provided by No 236 OCU, also at St Mawgan. In addition to submarine-hunting, the Nimrods conduct regular patrols of Britain's 200-mile territorial waters ('Tapestry' operations) and are called-upon to participate in SAR missions under the direction of Northern and Southern Maritime Air Region HQs at Pitreavie Castle, Rosyth, and Mt Batten, Plymouth, respectively.

Slower, but by no means a less welcome sight to those in peril on the sea, are the Sea King HAR3s of No 202 Squadron and Wessex HC2s of No 22 Squadron, both based at Finningley but operating detachments at nine coastal bases. Their personnel, many of whom have been presented with awards for remarkable feats of airmanship and courage in atrocious weather, receive instruction at the SAR Training Squadron, Valley, whilst pilots' Sea King conversion takes place at Culdrose on a couple of HAR3s attached to the Royal Navy's 706 Squadron.

No 18 Group also gained the RAF's Canberra force from No 1 Group in December 1982, this being based at Wyton and

Above:
No 18 Group crest.

Below:
In the absence of a dual-control Buccaneer, No 237 OCU at Honington uses Hunter T7As for pilot conversion. The aircraft is fitted with some Buccaneer systems to ease the transition task.
P. A. Jackson

comprising No 100 Squadron in the target facilities role; No 360 Sqaudron, a joint RAF-RN unit with jamming-equipped Canberra T17s for ECM training; No 1 Photographic Reconnaissance Unit flying Canberra PR9s on non-operational survey tasks; and No 231 OCU for training. The wartime role of the Canberra is visual maritime reconnaissance.

Top:
Pictured at 'high altitude' compared with their normal mode of operations, four Buccaneer S2Bs of No 208 Squadron exercise in close formation over Scotland. *BAe*

Above:
The Sea King HAR3 is Strike Command's long-range SAR helicopter, seen here demonstrating a typical rescue of a downed airman from his life-raft. Not all such operations are undertaken in fair weather, and crew members have received gallantry awards for persevering with missions in atrocious conditions. *Westland*

Left:
Used for shorter-range SAR operations than the Sea King — although under no less arduous conditions — are the Wessex HC2s of No 22 Squadron's six detached Flights.

Overseas Elements

Apart from Germany, the RAF's overseas elements are also included in Strike Command, these having been expanded of late in connection with maintenance of the Falklands garrison. The units at RAF Stanley, Port Stanley, are: No 23 Squadron providing air defence with its Phantom FGR2s; the SAR Sea Kings of 1564 Flight, No 202 Squadron; a Harrier GR3 detachement (1453 Flight) with aircraft provided by the Wittering wing but crewed by personnel from all the RAF's Harrier squadrons on a rotational basis; and a Chinook detachement (1310 Flight) similarly manned, with aircraft from Odiham.

Other units abroad include No 28 Squadron with Wessex HC2s in Hong Kong for SAR and support of the British forces stationed there; No 84 Squadron, also with Wessex, at the Sovereign Base of Akrotiri, Cyprus, providing logistic support for the United Nations forces on the island and SAR services for the fighter squadrons detached to Akrotiri's armament practice camp; and two flights in Belize, Central America. The latter country, although now independent, relies on Britain to provide defence against Guatemalan territorial ambitions, Strike Command contributing No 1417 Flight's four Harriers, a Puma detachment from No 33 Squadron at Odiham and a selection of RAF Regiment Rapier SAMs. The Command also maintains bases at Gibraltar, Ascension Island (half-way point on the Falkland Island run) and a training component at Goose Bay Labrador, to which aircraft are dispatched for low-level flying without the constraints of European regulations. A similar facility was used at Offutt AFB, Nebraska until the last Vulcan B2s were withdrawn.

Above:
Strike Command's six Hercules C(K)1 tankers remain committed to the Falkland Islands supply line and the Harrier and Phantom units based at Port Stanley. The refuelling hose installation is mounted in the cargo ramp.

Below:
A small Strike Command force is maintained in Belize, Central America, to dissuade invasion by neighbouring Guatemala. Apart from Pumas and Rapier SAMs, it includes the Harrier GR3s of No 1417 Flight. *L. T. Peacock*

Right:
Military Air Traffic Operations crest.

Non-Flying Branches

A further non-flying branch of Strike Command is the Military Air Traffic Operations (MATO) which is of group status and based at Hillingdon House, Uxbridge, where it is co-located with the Civil ATO. Administration is by a Joint Field Commander who is responsible for the joint implementation of National Air Traffic Services (NATS) policy for the control of civil and military aircraft in the United Kingdom. Associated with Strike Command for administrative purposes are two more units, of which the best-known is the Royal Observer Corps and its network of 870 observation posts not only for aircraft movements (as in World War 2) but also for monitoring nuclear fallout. The Central Trials and Tactics Organisation, also lodged at High Wycombe, is responsible for formulating tactical doctrine and conducting operational trials, for which it maintains a close liaison with the MoD research establishments and industry, and contacts with RAF operational commands, the Royal Navy, Army and Allied air forces. It is directly responsible to the Vice-Chief of Air Staff and the Commander-in-Chief for the conduct of trials and tactics development for all RAF operational aircraft and administers the Tornado Operational Evaluation Unit, formed at Boscombe Down on 1 September 1983 with four aircraft.

Costs

Running an air force is an expensive business, and Strike Command takes the lion's share of RAF operating costs in each year's defence budget. In 1983-84, Britain allocated £15,973million to defence, including £3,207million to RAF general purpose forces, £18million to the Auxiliaries, £274million to RAF training and £84million to air force war and contingency stocks, although the RAF also takes its share of the further cost devoted to research and development, repair and other support functions. Within the principal sum of £3,207million, an indication of priorities may be gained from the fact that £579million is devoted to air defence, £118million to offensive support, £922million to strike, attack and reconnaissance, £139million to maritime aircraft, £231million to transport aircraft, £128million to tankers, £17million to charter of civilian aircraft, £122million to other aircraft, £418million to operational stations, £68million to headquarters and £465million to general support, these sums comprising both purchase of new equipment and operating costs of that already in use.

In human assets, the RAF currently possesses a full-time strength of 92,300 personnel, including 87,000 men of whom 14,500 are officers. The number of qualified aircrew is not disclosed, neither is the proportion serving with Strike Command.

Above:
The cost of each flying hour by a modern military aircraft means that as much training as possible must take place in a simulator. Three Tornado simulators have been installed at TTTE, Cottesmore, where these instructors are monitoring crew performance from the associated control room. *RAF Official*

Strike Command Organisation

HQ Strike Command, RAF High Wycombe, Buckinghamshire; AOC-in-C (and CINCUKAIR): Air Chief Marshal Sir David Craig KCB, OBE, MA

No 1 Group, Strike Command HQ RAF Upavon, Wiltshire

Squadron	Aircraft type	Base	Role
1	Harrier GR3 (T4)	Wittering	Close support and tactical recce
6	Jaguar GR1 (T2)	Coltishall	Tactical strike and close support
7	Chinook HC1	Odiham	Tactical transport
9	Tornado GR1 (GR1T)	Honington	Interdictor-strike
10	VC10 C1	Brize Norton	Strategic transport
24	Hercules C1/C3	Lyneham	Transport
27	Tornado GR1 (GR1T)	Marham	Interdictor-strike
30	Hercules C1/C3	Lyneham	Transport

Squadron	Aircraft type	Base	Role
32	Andover C1/CC2 HS125 CC1/2/3 Gazelle HCC4	Hortholt	Communications
33	Puma HC1	Odiham	Tactical transport
41	Jaguar GR1 (T2)	Coltishall	Tactical recce and close support
47	Hercules C1/C3	Lyneham	Transport
50	Vulcan K2 (B2)	Waddington	Airborne refuelling
51	Nimrod R1	Wyton	Intelligence
54	Jaguar GR1 (T2)	Coltishall	Tactical strike and close support
55	Victor K2	Marham	Airborne refuelling
57	Victor K2	Marham	Airborne refuelling
70	Hercules C1/C3	Lyneham	Transport
72	Wessex HC2	Aldergrove	Tactical support
101	VC10 K2/K3	Brize Norton	Tanker-transport
115	Andover E3	Benson	Calibration
207	Devon C2	Northolt Turnhouse (Det 1) Wyton (Det 2)	Communications
617	Tornado GR1	Marham	Interdictor-strike
226 OCU	Jaguar GR1/T2	Lossiemouth	Pilot conversion
232 OCU	Victor K2	Marham	Crew conversion
233 OCU	Harrier GR3/T4/T4A	Wittering	Pilot conversion
240 OCU	Chinook HC1 Puma HC1	Odiham	Crew conversion
241 OCU	VC10 C1, BAe146 C1	Brize Norton	Crew conversion
242 OCU	Hercules C1/C3	Lyneham	Crew conversion
TTTE	Tornado GR1/GR1T Tornado GS/GT Tornado IS/IT	Cottesmore	Crew conversion
TWCU	Tornado GR1/GR1T	Honington	Weapons training
TQF	Wessex HCC4 Andover CC2	Benson	The Queen's Flight
ATF	Andover C1	Benson	Crew conversion
—	TriStar K1/K(C) 1	Brize Norton	Tanker-transport

No 11 Group, Strike Command HQ RAF Stanmore, Middlesex

Squadron	Aircraft type	Base	Role
5	Lightning F6 (F3/T5)	Binbrook	Air defence
8	Shackleton AEW2	Lossiemouth	Airborne early warning
11	Lightning F6 (F3/T5)	Binbrook	Air defence
25	Bloodhound 2 SAM	Barkston Heath (A Flt) Wyton (B Flt) Wattisham (C Flt)	Air defence
29	Phantom FGR2	Coningsby	Air defence
43	Phantom FG1	Leuchars	Air defence
56	Phantom FGR2	Wattisham	Air defence
85	Bloodhound 2 SAM	West Raynham (A Flt) North Coates (B Flt) Bawdsey (C Flt)	Air defence
111	Phantom FG1	Leuchars	Air defence
228 OCU	Phantom FGR2	Coningsby	Crew conversion
LTF	Lightning F3/T5/F6	Binbrook	Pilot conversion
LAF	Lightning F3/T5/F6	Binbrook	Reserve aircraft pool
1 TWU	Hawk T1 Jet Provost T4 Hunter F6A/T7/FGA9	Brawdy	Weapons training
2 TWU	Hawk T1	Chivenor	Weapons training
—	Nimrod AEW3	Waddington	Airborne early warning
—	F-4J Phantom	Wattisham	Air defence

Note that Nos 5, 11, 56, 85 and 111 Squadrons, plus Rapiers of Nos 27 and 48 Squadrons, RAF Regiment (Leuchars and Lossiemouth respectively) are under direct NATO control.

No 18 Group, Strike Command HQ RAF Northwood, Middlesex

Squadron	Aircraft type	Base	Role
12	Buccaneer S2B (Hunter T7)	Lossiemouth	Maritime strike
22	Wessex HC2	Finningley	SAR

Squadron	Aircraft type	Base	Role
		Chivenor (A Flt)	
		Leuchars (B Flt)	
		Valley (C Flt)	
		Leconfield (D Flt)	
		Manston (E Flt)	
		Coltishall (F Flt)	
42	Nimrod MR2	St Mawgan	Maritime patrol
100	Canberra B2/PR7/E15/TT18	Wyton	Target facilities
120	Nimrod MR2	Kinloss	Maritime patrol
201	Nimrod MR2	Kinloss	Maritime patrol
202	Sea King HAR3	Finningley	SAR
		Boulmer (A Flt)	
		Brawdy (B Flt)	
		Lossiemouth (D Flt)	
206	Nimrod MR2	Kinloss	Maritime patrol
208	Buccaneer S2B (Hunter T7)	Lossiemouth	Maritime strike
360	Canberra T17	Wyton	Target facilities
231 OCU	Canberra B2/T4	Wyton	Crew conversion
236 OCU	Nimrod MR2	St Mawgan	Crew conversion
237 OCU	Buccaneer S2A/S2B Hunter T7A (F6A, T8B)	Lossiemouth	Crew conversion
1 PRU	Canberra PR9	Wyton	Photo-survey
SARTS	Wessex HC2	Valley	Crew conversion

Abbreviations

ATF	Andover Training Flight	SARTS	Search and Rescue Training Squadron
LAF	Lightning Augmentation Flight	TTTE	Trinational Tornado Training Establishment
LTF	Lightning Training Flight	TWCU	Tornado Weapons Conversion Unit
OCU	Operational Conversion Unit	TWU	Tactical Weapons Unit
PRU	Photo Reconnaissance Unit		

Shadow Squadrons

The following conversion units are allocated a 'shadow' squadron identity. Those whose aircraft carry the squadron insignia in place of the OCU markings are indicated thus(*).

Unit	'Shadow'
236 OCU	38 Squadron
228 OCU*	64 Squadron
TWCU	45 Squadron
1 TWU*	79 and 234 Squadrons
2 TWU*	63 and 151 Squadrons

Wings

Some squadrons operating the same aircraft type from one base have a pooling arrangement.

Kinloss Wing Combining the Nimrod MR2s of Nos 120, 201 and 206 Squadrons.

Lyneham Transport Wing Combining Hercules C1s, C1Ps, C(K)1s and C3s of Nos 24, 30, 47 and 70 Squadrons, plus No 242 OCU.

In addition, three training units have no equipment of their own and loan aircraft from other units as required: No 232 OCU operates Victor K2s of Nos 55 and 57 Squadrons (although one aircraft of No 57 Squadron is marked in OCU colours); No 241 OCU operates VC10s of No 10 Squadron and VC10 K2s; the SARTS uses Wessex HC2s of No 22 Squadron.

Secondary aircraft types and marks are shown in parentheses.

Strike Command Overseas

RAF flying units overseas (apart from those assigned to RAF Germany) are administered by Strike Command.

Squadron	Aircraft Type	Base	Role
23	Phantom FGR2	Stanley, Falkland Is	Air defence
28	Wessex HC2	Sek Kong, Hong Kong	SAR and support
84	Wessex HC2	Akrotiri, Cyprus	SAR and United Nations support
1564 Flight	Sea King HAR3	Stanley, Falkland Is	SAR and support
1417 Flight	Harrier GR3	Belize City, Belize	Ground attack
1453 Flight	Harrier GR3	Stanley, Falkland Is	Close support and air defence
1310 Flight	Chinook HC1	Stanley, Falkland Is	Tactical transport
1312 Flight	Hercules C(K)1	Stanley, Falkland Is	Refuelling/Sea Patrol
Puma Det	Puma HC1	Belize City, Belize	Tactical transport

The Royal Air Force Regiment

Formed on 1 February 1942 by Royal Charter (the only RAF component to be thus brought into being) the Regiment initially assumed the roles of Army troops stationed at British airfields for defensive duties, and rapidly expanded to a peak strength of 90,000 men — almost the size of the entire RAF today. A corps in its own right, it is nevertheless an integral part of the air force structure, forming together with the RAF Police and Fire Service, the Security Branch of the RAF. Overall control is vested in the person of the Commandant General and Director General of Security, although the wing commander responsible for Regiment units in Britain (other components are allocated to RAF Germany) is directly subordinate to the AOC-in-C, Strike Command.

The principal brief of the Regiment is to provide RAF airfields with the means to survive enemy air and ground attacks in order that air operations may continue for as long as possible, and for this task it is equipped with both missiles and surface weapons. Organisation employs RAF terms — a flight being equivalent to an army platoon, a squadron equating to a company, and a wing loosely matching a battalion.

Defence against air attack is mainly entrusted to the two squadrons of Rapier SAMs attached to bases in Scotland, whilst four ground defence squadrons are stationed at Hullavington and Catterick and are available for deployment elsewhere, as required. Rapier units, known as SHORAD (SHOrt Range Air Defence) Squadrons, deploy outside the boundaries of their home base to protect it against intruding aircraft which have eluded the manned interceptor forces. Some Auxiliary personnel are now being enlisted on a trial basis.

Since August 1981, light armoured squadrons have been equipped with Scorpion reconnaissance vehicles (mounting a 76mm gun) and Spartan armoured troop carriers, as well as in smaller numbers, Sultan command vehicles and Samson recovery vehicles. Acting as the 'eyes and ears' of airfield defence, they would be deployed well outside the perimeter fence and engage any hostile force attempting to over-run the base.

Small detachments of Regiment personnel are present at each RAF station to train personnel in the use of small arms and advise on other defensive aspects such as protection against NBC (Nuclear, Biological and Chemical) attack, but additional security is now being provided for Strike Command by part-time forces. In 1979, the Regiment formed the first of an eventual 20 or more Auxiliary Field Squadrons, six of which are currently in being, equipped with light armoured vehicles.

Lesser-known RAF Regiment components include the three Maritime Headquarters Units which provide staff for the Northern and Southern Maritime Air Region HQs and additionally exercise with maritime forces in such overseas locations as Gibraltar. There is also an Auxiliary Air Movements Squadron in the process of formation with a planned strength of 400 personnel organised into mobile teams. This unique unit formed at Brize Norton on 2 August 1982.

Under the terms of an agreement negotiated with the US Air Force, the Regiment will man Rapiers purchased with American funds for defence of USAF bases in Britain. For administrative reasons the new squadrons will be stationed at RAF airfields, deploying to US bases as required. The first unit formed at West Raynham, Norfolk, in November 1983, to be followed by squadrons at Brize Norton in 1984 and Honington in 1986.

Above:
Members of the RAF Regiment using laser targeting equipment.
RAF Official

RAF Regiment Squadrons Assigned to Strike Command

SHORAD Squadrons

27	Leuchars
48	Lossiemouth

(Both squadrons under direct NATO control)

Field Squadrons

2	Hullavington
15	Hullavington
51	Catterick
58	Catterick
2503 (Aux)	'County of Lincoln'
2620 (Aux)	'County of Norfolk'
2622 (Aux)	'Highland'
2623 (Aux)	'East Anglian'
2624 (Aux)	'County of Oxford'
2625 (Aux)	'County of Cornwall'

Regiment Depot

Catterick

Air Movements Squadron

4624 (Aux)	'County of Oxford'

Maritime Headquarters Units

1	'County of Hertford'
2	'City of Edinburgh'
3	'County of Devon'

Left:
Airfield protection by the Regiment in very different environments: guarding a Harrier during an exercise in Scotland, and . . .

Below left:
. . . No 34 Squadron in Akrotiri, Cyprus. *Both: RAF Official*

Below right:
RAF Regiment insignia. *P. A. Jackson*

Bottom:
The RAF Regiment's light armoured squadrons use the CVR(T) family — Scorpion light tanks, Samson ARVs and (as pictured here) Spartan APCs. *MoD*

4. WEAPONRY

The undoubted efficiency with which Strike Command undertakes its assigned tasks is a product of quality, both in men and equipment, and the reputation for excellence which the RAF has gained throughout the world has been achieved by a long-sustained policy of obtaining only the best that available resources can secure. In any discussion of weaponry, therefore, first mention must be given to the human resources of the Command. Exceptional ability in an aircraft may be able to obviate some shortcomings in the men who fly and maintain it, but the trade-off is very small and serious problems are in store for any air force which fails to ensure that both men and machines are to the same high standard.

As an all-volunteer force, the RAF already has a significant advantage over air arms in countries where conscription is still the rule, and although government restrictions on pay have periodically depressed recruitment, the challenge of a career in close contact with high technology has usually been sufficient to ensure an ample supply of suitable applicants for air and ground positions. Reflecting the highly technical nature of flying today, a great proportion of RAF officers are university graduates, and what were previously regarded as the mundane tasks of the non-commissioned airman are now equally demanding of specialised training. Most importantly of all, however, the RAF has devised methods of instilling Service discipline into its personnel whilst simultaneously developing their initiative and self-reliance. This is a finely balanced procedure, yet one which gives British fliers a clear superiority over their counterparts in the Warsaw Pact, where to think for oneself is to question the absolute authority of the State and invite the attendant penalties. Even within NATO, few air forces can equal the RAF's reputation for flexibility of tactics and adaptability at relatively junior level.

Tornado

The quest for excellence is presently expressing itself in delivery of the world's most advanced interdictor-strike aircraft to the RAF. Panavia's Tornado, developed in conjunction with West Germany and Italy, is a prime example of sound international collaboration between allies, and an aeroplane which has been 'right' from the moment of its conception. Though delayed in introduction to service, the Tornado has been well worth waiting for, and its two versions will equip a sizeable proportion of Strike Command in the 1990s.

Development of what was then known as the MRCA (Multi-Role Combat Aircraft) began in the late 1960s with the coming together of BAC (later part of BAe) and Messerschmitt-Bölkow (now MBB) after each had unsuccessfully pursued similar projects with other partners. More NATO countries expressed interest and then dropped out, but when Panavia GmbH was formed in March 1969 to manage the MRCA programme, it comprised BAC, MBB and Aeritalia, with Germany having design leadership by virtue of

its requirement for 700 aircraft. Needs changed when the Luftwaffe was partially re-equipped with Phantoms, and Britain is now the major customer with 385, followed by 324 for Germany (including 112 to be used by the naval air arm) and 100 for Italy.

The first of 15 development MRCAs was airborne on 14 August 1974 in Germany and, after the usual service trials, crew training for all four users began in January 1981 prior to the first deliveries to operational units in mid-1982. Tornado IDS — interdictor-strike — is the basic version in operation by every customer, 220 being on order for RAF as the Tornado GR1 and GR1T dual-control model. Built to exacting standards and powered by two purpose-designed Turbo Union RB199 reheated turbofan engines rated at up to 16,800lb st in their present Mk 103 form, the Tornado GR1 is capable of carrying the full spectrum of weaponry operated by each of its users — no mean achievement in itself.

For the RAF this means nuclear, cluster or 1,000lb bombs (free-fall, laser-guided or retarded); two AIM-9L Sidewinders

for self-defence; and newly-ordered equipment of an advanced nature. Now in the trials stage, the Hunting JP233 pod is a dispenser of area-denial bomblets, two of which will be positioned under the Tornado's belly to endow it with exceptional capability in the counter-air (anti-airfield) role. Air Staff Targets 1227 and 1228 call for an anti-armour weapon and an anti-radiation missile to provide the aircraft with an ability to destroy hostile radar positions in the defence-suppression mode. BAe Dynamics offered the ALARM (Air-Launched Anti-Radiation Missile) for this latter task and the US company Texas Instruments put in a counter-proposal with the AGM-88 HARM (High-speed ARM). A decision in favour of the ALARM was announced in mid-1983.

Despite its size (fuselage length is shorter than the Phantom) the Tornado carries a remarkable array of avionics to ensure accurate weapons' delivery, and in evidence externally are up to two Marconi ARI 23246/1 Sky Shadow jamming pods mounted on the outboard wing pylons and a laser designator beneath the forward fuselage of aircraft produced from Batch 3 onwards (79th GR1), this to be retrospectively fitted to all. The usual radar warning receiver is installed in the fin, whilst the nose radome covers a highly accurate radar with an automatic terrain-following mode which will fly the aircraft 'hands off' 200ft above the ground at night and in all weathers. No other aircraft will rival this ability until the very much larger Rockwell B-1B enters service later this decade, and it says much for the Tornado's allied navigation equipment that aircraft have returned to base after an hour's flying of complex patterns at low level with a total nav systems error of 60ft — the length of the average back garden! This and a weapons-aiming computer which automatically releases stores after compensation for variables such as cross-wind, explains the Tornado crews' unbounded enthusiasm for their aircraft.

Buccaneer

Previously assigned to similar low-level strike duties, the Buccaneer S2B is now transferring its still considerable talents to the anti-shipping role. Designed during the early 1950s for operation from aircraft carriers, the Buccaneer is another aircraft which was in the vanguard of aeronautical progress

Three Buccaneer S2Bs of No 208 Squadron break to starboard over the snow-covered Scottish Highlands during a training exercise. Two practice bombs are carried in each of the carriers on the outer wing pylons. *BAe*

during early service, its tasks demanding strides forward in aerodynamics and new techniques of milling structural components from the solid to provide the immense strength necessary to resist the severe stresses imposed by low-altitude flight. Despite these measures, Buccaneers were grounded for six months in 1980 with fatigue cracks in some aircraft, and not all have returned to flying duties; yet so strong is crew members' affection for the agile Buccaneer that posting to a Tornado squadron is regarded by many as a disastrous move, whatever the latter's advantage in 'clever black boxes'.

Providing a stable weapons platform at relatively high speeds, the Buccaneer has been operated in the overland strike role since it joined the RAF in 1969, with up to four cluster bombs (CBUs) or parachute-retarded bombs in the rotating weapons bay, and a fifth beneath the wing, with the remaining external strongpoints mounting two fuel tanks and a Westinghouse AN/ALQ-101-10 jamming pod. Buccaneers of RAF Germany carried a single AIM-9B Sidewinder in place of the fifth bomb, and this has appeared on UK-based aircraft. Anti-shipping roles involve the Buccaneer carrying Martel missiles in their anti-radiation or TV-guided forms, or laser-guided bombs (LCBs) and their associated Pave Spike designator in a wing-mounted pod. Retained for maritime duties until the 1990s, Buccaneers will be fitted with BAeD P3T Sea Eagle surface-skimming missiles (produced to ASR 1226 as a Martel replacement) and airframe improvements including an updated nav/attack system and chaff dispensers.

Tornado ADV

It is necessary to return once more to the Tornado to discuss air defence equipment, for this versatile aircraft is to be the principal Strike Command interceptor from the latter half of the 1980s until well into the next century. The Tornado F2 — or Air Defence Variant (ADV) — is an adaptation of the basic aircraft specifically to RAF requirements, the longer fuselage for additional fuel capacity incidentally endowing it with better manoeuvrability than its interdictor companion, although the two otherwise have 80% of their components in common. To place the Tornado F2's agility in perspective, however, it must be remembered that RAF requirements are for a long-range 'bomber-killer' rather than a lightweight dogfighter, and thus no claims are made that the aircraft is in the F-16 class of manoeuvrability. The vital factor in the F2's case is that at an early stage in trials — begun with the first flight of one of the three prototypes on 27 October 1979 — it demonstrated the ability to fly at a speed of 800kts at low level, this being a useful 50-100kts above the structural or aerodynamic limits of potential targets at that altitude.

Armament of the Tornado F2 will comprise four BAeD Skyflash radar-guided missiles partially recessed into the belly; an infra-red seeking AIM-9L Sidewinder on each inboard wing pylon; and a single, internal 27mm Mauser cannon (compared with two carried by the GR1). Sky Flash is a British development of the Sparrow featuring indigenous guidance and fusing mechanisms, whilst the AIM-9L comes from a NATO programme involving assembly of British, German, Italian and Norwegian components by Bodenseewerke of West Germany. Development of a Sky Flash Mk 2 was halted for economy reasons in 1981, but the Mk 1 weapon will eventually be replaced by the Hughes AIM-120 AMRAAM (Advanced Medium Range Air-Air Missile) built under licence in Europe. As part of the same agreement with the USA, European firms are designing an Advanced Short Range AAM to replace the Sidewinder on both sides on the Atlantic, and this too, will become part of the weapons fit of the 165 Tornado F2s due to enter service from early 1985 onwards.

Above:
The prototype Tornado F2 displays its normal operational load of four semi-recessed Sky Flashes beneath the fuselage, a Sidewinder on the inside edge of the wing pylons and two fuel tanks. *BAe*

Below:
The Tornado F2's fully-retracting refuelling probe was tested early in the flight-trials programme by Strike Command Victor K2s from Marham. In this instance the donor is from No 55 Squadron, as evidenced by the insignia of a hand clutching a spear, all in blue. *BAe*

Nimrod AEW

Assisting the Tornado F2 in acquisition of its targets will be the Nimrod AEW3, 11 of which are being converted from MR1 standard. Development of the AEW3 was authorised in March 1977 after Britain withdrew from the NATO planning group which was at that time discussing (and discussing) a multinational AEW force. The latter ultimately decided on the Boeing E-3A Sentry which, due to production already in hand, arrived in Europe before the Nimrod Mk 3 was available to the RAF.

Designed to track ships as well as low-flying aircraft over land or sea and operate in spite of electronic jamming, the Nimrod AEW3 relies on three main sensors collectively known as the Mission System Avionics. Most obvious of these are two radar scanners mounted fore and aft to give an uninterrupted coverage of the earth and obviate the fuselage blanking effect suffered by the Sentry's parasol radome. Radar is of the multimode pulse-doppler type which utilises the changed frequency of reflections from moving targets to enable low-altitude aircraft to be detected, even in the presence of strong ground returns. The rate at which pulses are transmitted can be varied to maximise detection, and by interleaving the available modules the system can simultaneously plot both aircraft and comparatively slow-moving ships.

Wingtip pods contain a passive radio and radar detection system (Electronic Support Measures, or ESM), whilst an IFF — Identification Friend or Foe — interrogator checks targets for the coded radio response which will classify them as friendly. Inputs from all these sensors are fed into the data handling system together with information from the Nimrod's navigation equipment, and can be selected as required by the six-man tactical team. The latter comprises a tactical air control officer, communications officer, ESM operator and three air direction officers who work at adjacent positions in the forward fuselage of the aircraft.

Below:
The Nimrod AEW3 will be a central feature of Britain's air defences until well into the next century, its bulbous nose and tail containing radars designed to track low-flying intruders as well as shipping. This, the first production AEW3, does not carry the in-flight refuelling probe which will be retrospectively fitted to the type. *BAe*

Right:
The six-man tactical team housed in the Nimrod AEW3's fuselage operates a bewildering array of computer keyboards and switches forming part of the Mission System Avionics. Main inputs are from the radar, ESM and IFF interrogator, working in conjunction with the aircraft's highly accurate navigation system. *BAe*

Trials of the Nimrod's radar began in June 1977 when the nose component became airborne for the first time in a specially modified Comet, whilst the first of three Nimrods converted for development work was flown on 16 July 1980, this being an aerodynamic testbed without any hardware inside the radomes. Eight more conversions will follow before the three trials aircraft return to the works for full modification to Service standards, and all will have refuelling probes for extended operations.

Lightning

In terms of seniority, Strike Command's interceptor forces are led by the BAC Lightning — perhaps the last wholly-British fighter to serve the RAF. The Lightning's story began in 1947 with issue of a specification for a high-speed research aircraft, three of which were ordered from what was then English Electric on 1 April 1950. The first of these flew on 4 August 1954 and three more prototypes and 20 development aircraft followed before the Lightning F1 entered service in 1960, progressing through F1A and F2 marks before the square-finned F3 and F6 appeared with de Havilland Red Top infra-red missiles in place of the earlier Firestreak weapon.

The first truly supersonic RAF interceptor, the Lightning served both at home and overseas, those allocated to Germany being converted to F6 standard as the F2A before replacement by Phantoms in 1977. Only the F6 now remains in quantity service, supported by a small number of F3s and compatible T5 two-seat trainers, and although the aircraft is under-armed compared with some fighters (two 30mm Aden cannon in the F6 and two Firestreaks or Red Tops on all versions), those who have been privileged to witness an aerobatic display will agree that the aircraft is still remarkably sprightly for its age.

Phantom

By the mid-1970s the Lightning's status as the principal RAF interceptor had been assumed by the McDonnell Douglas Phantom, an aircraft designed for the US Navy in the early 1950s and subsequently adopted by air arms around the world. British deliveries totalled 52 F-4K Phantom FG1s for the Fleet Air Arm and 118 F-4M Phantom FGR2s for the RAF, some of the former transferring to Strike Command immediately afterwards due to reductions in the Navy carrier strength. Phantom FGR2s began arriving in July 1968, with several of the early squadrons taking up station in Germany in the strike role until they could be replaced by Jaguars in 1975 and their aircraft reassigned to home air defence. FG1s operated in the latter role from September 1969, the RAF taking over the last of the Navy's FG1s in 1978. Four Phantom squadrons, two of them home-based, will be retained for as long as their airframe hours permit after the Tornado F2 is fully deployed.

British Phantoms are unique in their employment of two Rolls-Royce Spey afterburning turbojets in place of General Electric J79s used by other variants, a stipulation made in order to reduce foreign expenditure. Despite the outstanding qualities of both airframe and engine, this marriage proved less than happy in its early stages, and although problems have been overcome, the F-4K and F-4M remain slightly slower than other marks of Phantom. The aircraft is nevertheless well equipped for its role, originally carrying four radar-homing AIM-7E2 Sparrows semi-recessed beneath the fuselage and four AIM-9D/G Sidewinders on dual wing pylons. Later models of these weapons are now becoming available in the forms of AIM-9L and Sky Flash, whilst a podded SUU-20 rapid-firing cannon can also be fitted on the centreline.

Harrier

Of all Strike Command's aircraft, perhaps none has caught the public imagination more than the Harrier and its unique vertical take-off capability. Symbolising British expertise and determination, today's Harrier evolved from a purely experimental design of the late 1950s which was originally pursued by Hawker Aircraft and Bristol Siddeley Engines in the face of official indifference. Indeed, it is to the engine manufacturer that credit should be given for the Harrier, its Pegasus engine with four swivelling nozzles providing a fundamental breakthrough at a time when VTOL aircraft on other manufacturers' drawing boards featured banks of vertically-mounted lifting engines which were only so much dead weight for all except a few moments of flying time.

The first of six prototype Hawker P1127s — as the aircraft was initially known — made a tethered hover on 21 October 1960 and thanks to American and German interest, nine semi-militarised Kestrel variants were operated during 1964-65 on operational trials to test the viability of VTOL in the offensive role. Each nation then went its own way, Britain proposing to build an advanced combat aircraft, the P1154, on the vertical take-off principle until politics and financial problems intervened. Instead, the P1127 was extensively re-engineered as the Harrier and six development aircraft were ordered prior to the award of production contracts eventually totalling 118 single-seat close-support variants and 23 trainers. All of these had been supplied by the end of 1983 except for four required as replacements for losses in the Falklands war.

The early Harrier GR1 progressively became the GR1A and GR3 as engine power increased, trainers likewise being upgraded from T2 to T2A and T4, although the T4A is a specially lightened version lacking the nose-mounted LRMTS (laser ranger and marked target seeker). Deliveries of production Harriers began in 1969, Strike Command forming an OCU and one squadron before the remainder were allocated to RAF Germany. A typical weapons' load for the Harrier GR3 — using a short take-off run — would comprise two podded 30mm Aden cannon beneath the fuselage and a BL755 cluster bomb on each of the outboard wings pylons, plus fuel tanks inboard, but this may be varied with 1,000lb bombs (free-fall, retarded or laser-guided), SNEB 68mm rocket pods and the additional armament adopted for the Falklands war: Royal Navy 2in rocket pods and self-defence Sidewinders. Additional operational protection has been provided recently in the form of Marconi Zeus internal jamming equipment and a chaff/flare dispenser immediately to the rear of the belly airbrake. Future plans include wingtip Sidewinder installation in order that valuable weapons pylons can be released to carry offensive stores. An improved version of the BL755 has recently been ordered.

Below left:
Pre-flight checks. Flt Lt Mark Hare of No 1 Squadron examines his Harrier GR3 at Ascension Island before embarking *Atlantic Conveyor* for the passage south to the Falkland Islands. *BAe*

Bottom left:
Arming a Harrier with a SNEB rocket pod. *RAF Official*

Below:
Three Harrier GR3s of No 1 Squadron are seen on board HMS *Hermes* in June 1982, together with Sea Harriers and a Sea King. The aircraft in the foreground carries laser-guided bombs on the outboard pylons. *RAF Official*

Jaguar

Also used for close support, the SEPECAT Jaguar GR1 is an Anglo-French design produced by the former BAC and Breguet companies for their respective air arms. First flown in France on 8 September 1968 and in Britain on 12 October 1969, the aircraft was ordered for the RAF in single-seat form as the Jaguar S, or GR1 (165 built), and the two-seat Jaguar B, T2 (35 aircraft), a further three of the latter also having been acquired for MoD establishments. Service operation began in May 1973 with first deliveries to the OCU, and now in addition to three operational squadrons of Strike Command a further five units are stationed in Germany.

For a small aircraft, the Jaguar is remarkably well armed, its two internal 30mm Aden cannon being augmented by up to eight 1,000lb bombs or BL755 CBUs for short-range operations: two under the fuselage, two on tanden inboard pylons and one on each outer position, although four bombs and two inboard fuel tanks are the norm. Where laser designation facilities are available from another aircraft or the ground, the Jaguar can also release Pave Way bombs with the usual unerring accuracy or rely on its own nose-mounted LRMTS for delivery of unguided ordnance. In addition to the Marconi ARI 18223 E-J band RWR which it shares with Harriers, Jaguar has received additional equipment for self-defence, a chaff dispenser in the tailcone parachute housing having been recently boosted by optional installations of Sidewinders, AN/ALQ-101 jamming pods and Philips-MATRA Phimat chaff/flare dispenser pods. These again occupy pylon space, and it is proposed to fit the aircraft with additional attachment points for missiles and jammers — of a type yet to be decided in the last-mentioned case. Improvement of the Jaguar's nav/attack equipment began in 1983 with a retrofit programme for the Ferranti FIN 1064 intertial navigation system, representing a smaller, lighter yet far more capable aid to the pilot than that available when the aircraft was designed. Orders have been placed for 100 sets of FIN 1064, and Strike Command's Coltishall wing will be the first to benefit.

Above:

Jaguar conversion training is provided by No 226 OCU at Lossiemouth with GR Mk 1s (illustrated) and T Mk 2s. Unit markings on the air intake comprise a torch and a quiver of arrows indicating the two aspects of the OCU's task: instruction and offensive operations. *P. A. Jackson*

Below:

Ground crew must be capable of servicing aircraft whilst dressed in NBC protective clothing, as demonstrated by these personnel attaching a BL755 cluster-bomb to the outer pylon of a Jaguar GR1 st Coltishall during a Taceval. *RAF*

Nimrod MR

In the maritime role, surveillance tasks are undertaken by the Nimrod MR2 and its sophisticated array of sensing equipment. Originating from an RAF requirement for a Shackleton replacement, the Nimrod traces its ancestry back to the de Havilland Comet (the world's first jet airliner) which, with the addition of a lower 'bubble' to the fuselage, flew as the prototype Nimrod MR1 on 23 May 1967. The first of an initial batch of 38 aircraft entered service in October 1969 and a further eight were ordered — some of which remained with Hawker Siddeley (later BAe) at Woodford for trials work. A further contract covered three elint (*electronic intelligence*) Nimrod R1s, delivered from July 1971 and extensively modified by the RAF before they began operations in May 1974. These lack the distinctive extended MAD tailboom.

Of 46 Nimrod MR1s, 11 are being converted to AEW3 standard whilst the remainder have been returned to Woodford for updating to MR2s. This involves the replacement of the original ASV-21 radar by the much improved Searchwater; the addition of AQS-901 acoustics processing equipment and associated Australian-designed Barra sonobuoys; and (yet to be fitted) Loral ESM equipment in the wingtip pods. Some indication of the MR2's enhanced capabilities is provided by the fact that it possesses 60 times the computer power of its predecessor, giving the 10-man tactical team in the fuselage far greater scope for dealing with tracking situations. Nimrod MR2s entered service in August 1979 and all will have completed conversion by the end of 1984.

The Nimrod's long weapons bay houses a wide variety of mines, depth charges, bombs and homing torpedoes, the last-mentioned including the new Stingray. Single strong points under each wing were included in the design for anti-ship missiles, but in the event these remained unoccupied by the Aérospatiale AS-12s and HSD Martels for which they were provided. In 1982, however, the Nimrod MR2 was rapidly reconfigured for the Falklands war and received a pair of self-defence Sidewinders on each wing, and stowage in the weapons bay for the McDonnell Douglas Harpoon anti-ship missile — carried for the first time by an RAF aircraft. These options have been retained. In-flight refuelling capacity was also added in 1982 in the form of a receiver probe above the cockpit and a small ventral fin at the rear for aerodynamic compensation.

Strike Command's remaining armament comprises the Bloodhound and Rapier SAMs and the helicopters which may be equipped with a light machine gun in the cabin doorway, but it would be no exaggeration to claim that even unarmed aircraft are also a highly effective weapon. The Hercules and VC-10s moving men and equipment swiftly to the scene of tension or conflict; Canberras sharpening the wits of fighter controllers and interceptor crews; Andovers ensuring the safe all-weather operation of airfields; tankers keeping thirsty aircraft on station or expediting their deployment overseas; light transport ensuring rapid liaison between key personnel — all are crucial to the functioning of Strike Command as a well-designed and smoothly-operating single weapon in Britain's hands.

Having just been converted from Mk 1 standard, Strike Command's Nimrod MR2s received further modifications during 1982 in the form of an in-flight refuelling probe and provision for Sidewinders beneath the wings. This aircraft wears the latest hemp upper surface camouflage which is unusual in featuring hybrid national insignia: Type B fuselage roundels and fin flashes, with Type D roundels beneath the wings.   *BAe*

CHRONOLOGY OF STRIKE COMMAND AIRCRAFT

Aircraft	Chronology
ANDOVER	+ ======= XXXXXXXXXXXXXXXXXXXXXXXXXXXXXXXXXXXXXXX
BAe 146	++++ X
BUCCANEER	++++++ ================== XXXXXXXXXXXXXXXXXXXXXXXXXXXXXX
CANBERRA	++ XXXXXXXXXXXXXXXXXXXXXXXXXXXXXXXXXXXXXXXXXXXXXXXXXXXXXXXXXX
CHINOOK	++ == XXXXXXXXX
DEVON (Dove)	++ ==== XXXXXXXXXXXXXXXXXXXXXXXXXXXXXXXXXXXXXXXXXXXXXXXXXXXXXXXXXX
HARRIER	P1127 +++++++++++++++++++++ XXXXXXXXXXXXXXXXXXXXXXXXXXXXXXX
HAWK	++++ XXXXXXXXXXXXXXXXXX
HERCULES	+++========================= XXXXXXXXXXXXXXXXXXXXXXXXXXXXXXXXXXX
HS 125	++++ ================ XXXXXXXXXXXXXXXXXXXXXXXXXXXXXXX
GAZELLE	+++++++++++++ == XXXXXXXXXXXXXXXXXXXXXXXXXXX
HUNTER	+++++++ XXXXXXXXXXXXXXXXXXXXXXXXXXXXXXXXXXXXXXXXXXXXXXXXXXXXXX
JAGUAR	+++++++++++ XXXXXXXXXXXXXXXXXXXXXXXXXX
JET PROVOST	++ XXXXXXXXXXXXXXXXXXXXXXXXXXXXXXXXXXXXXXXXXXXXXXXXXXXXXXXX
LIGHTNING	P1 ++++++++++++ XXXXXXXXXXXXXXXXXXXXXXXXXXXXXXXXXXXXXXXXXXXX
NIMROD	++++ XXXXXXXXXXXXXXXXXXXXXXXXXXXXXXXXXX
PHANTOM	++++++ ================ XXXXXXXXXXXXXXXXXXXXXXXXXXXXXXXX
PUMA	+++++++++ ==== XXXXXXXXXXXXXXXXXXXXXXXXXXX
SHACKLETON	++++ XXXXXXXXXXXXXXXXXXXXXXXXXXXXXXXXXXXXXXXXXXXXXXXXXXXXXX
TORNADO	+++++++++++++ XXXXXXXXX
TRISTAR	+++++================================ X
SEA KING	S-61 ++++ == XXXXXXXXXX
VC10	++ ======= XXXXXXXXXXXXXXXXXXXXXXXXXXXXXXXX
VICTOR	++++++++++++ XXXXXXXXXXXXXXXXXXXXXXXXXXXXXXXXXXXXXXXXXXXXXX
VULCAN	+++++++++++ XXXXXXXXXXXXXXXXXXXXXXXXXXXXXXXXXXXXXXXXXXXXXX
WESSEX	(S-58) ++ ================== XXXXXXXXXXXXXXXXXXXXXXXXXXXXXXX

| 1945 | 1950 | 1955 | 1960 | 1965 | 1970 | 1975 | 1980 | 1984 |

KEY: FIRST FLIGHT ++++++++++++++++   ENTERED OTHER SERVICE========   ENTERED RAF SERVICE XXXXXXXXX

Maintenance of Strike Command's high level of operational competence is achieved through unceasing rehearsal and training at all levels, from a pair of fighters participating in mock combat to large-scale manoeuvres involving the land, sea and air forces of several NATO countries. It is through such efforts that existing tactics are perfected and new ones evolved, ensuring that at all times the RAF is fully conversant with the latest state of the air warfare art.

Because of fuel and maintenance costs, flying time is restricted — NATO standards calling for a minimum of 180 hours for combat pilots each year, equivalent to perhaps just one hour per day, taking into account holidays, weekends and courses — and thus every minute in the air must be used to full advantage. On the day he reports for duty with his first squadron, a young combat pilot has already received £2million worth of training, but this is only the beginning of a career during which he may expect to fly several types of aircraft in differing roles and must be thoroughly au fait with all their characteristics and capabilities.

For the submarine-hunting Nimrods and the fighter units which intercept Soviet reconnaissance aircraft, contact with the potential adversary is a daily occurrence. The transport squadrons are also regularly employed in air movements; yet even so, these duties do not allow RAF units to practice their full repertoire of required skills — regular realistic training is necessary. For the interceptors this involves air combat manoeuvring with their own kind, strike aircraft and occasionally the USAF 'aggressor' squadron of F-5Es (527th TFTAS) which is based at Alconbury and specialises in emulating Soviet combat tactics. This is augmented by gunnery exercises against towed targets, interception of jamming-equipped Canberra T17s (to improve radar techniques) and missile firing camp at Valley, whilst at least one deployment is made yearly to the armament practice base at

The RAF received 14 VC10 C1s between 1966 and 1968, of which 13 remain (the other having been used for RB211 engine development). Each is individually named after a VC of the air, XR807 being in joint memory of D. E. Garland, VC and T. Gray, VC. *MoD*

Above:
Sea King HAR3s based in the Falkland Islands with No 1564 Flight have changed their normal yellow SAR colours to a coat of overall matt dark Admiralty grey with Type B (without white) roundels. *P. A. Jackson*

Left:
Also part of the South Atlantic fit for Sea King HAR3s is a radar warning receiver (RWR) with aerials on the extreme nose, as shown, and beneath the tailboom. *P. A. Jackson*

Below:
Fetching and carrying for the Army is the principal task of the Strike Command battlefield helicopter force. Wessex HC2s of No 18 Squadron are here taking part in NATO Exercise 'Amber Express' in Denmark during 1981, although they have now been withdrawn from the Continental reinforcement role.
P. A. Jackson

Right:
Harriers in hiding. No 1 Squadron's Harrier GR3s have the unique ability to operate from short fields or lengths of road, refuelling and rearming being accomplished in camouflaged hides nearby. Strips of aluminium planking prevent the aircraft from becoming bogged-down in the waterlogged ground, whilst a refuelling hose in the background is linked to flexible bulk storage bags. *P. A. Jackson*

Below:
Hardened aircraft shelters are a novel experience for No 6 Squadron's Jaguar GR1s when taking part in exercises on the Continent, and provide useful training for ground crews not accustomed to working in such claustrophobic conditions.
P. A. Jackson

Akrotiri in Cyprus. Varying scales of national air defence exercises are held, but two or three times per year the 'Priory' series involves NATO and French aircraft mounting raids on Britain to test the complete defence organisation.

Strike aircraft pilots maintain their skills by regular sorties to the weapons ranges around the coast and at remote inland locations, probably including precision navigation and fighter affiliation in the same sorties to use their time profitably. Whenever possible, they participate in the regular 'Mallet Blow' exercises on the Otterburn range in Northumberland, fighters and SAMs adding extra realism to the operation. USAF units are also invited to take part, and by way of reciprocation, a lucky few RAF units are allowed to join in the highly authentic 'Red Flag' exercises in the Nevada desert. Within Europe, detachments are made to the NATO range at Decimomannu, Sardinia, whilst Jaguars, Harriers, Pumas, Chinooks, Hercules and VC10s are all involved in the major exercises which NATO regularly undertakes to test its rapid deployment plans to such places as Denmark. Winter training detachments to Norway involve Jaguars, Harriers and helicopters replacing the grey of their camouflage with white for improved concealment.

For all these exercises, plans are made well in advance and care is taken to ensure that every facet of the operation proceeds as intended. No such luxury is enjoyed during a Taceval (tactical evaluation) which is undertaken on a station basis, and the first sign of the exercise is a team of examiners marching into the base operations block to announce that 'the war' has started. From that moment onwards, every unit on the station assumes its wartime role, recalling personnel from their homes (if it is after normal working hours), guarding key points against sabotage, launching combat sorties and taking precautions against NBC (nuclear, biological and chemical) attack. Every conceivable aspect of performance is monitored by the scrutineers, who make the situation as realistic as possible by introducing damage, unserviceability and casualties as the exercise progresses, and a full report is later made to the station commander so that he can take action to remedy any weaknesses.

Such attention to detail paid handsome dividends when Strike Command was called into action with the Argentine invasion of the Falkland Islands on 2 April 1982 and predetermined war plans had to be drastically modified to take account of the vast distance to the operational area. As usual, it was the transport force of Hercules and VC10s which was called into action first, to begin positioning supplies and equipment at the mid-way staging point of Ascension Island, and in an effort sustained over three months the transports flew over 17,000 hours and carried 7,000 tons, including nearly 100 vehicles and over 20 helicopters. Early loads comprised personnel to operate the forward base and greatly expand its communications and aircraft servicing facilities.

Protection of the Task Force at sea was entrusted to the Nimrods which kept watch for submarines and supported the efforts of the naval ASW helicopters on their unceasing patrols. At a later stage the same aircraft reconnoitred the exclusion zone around the islands, assisted aircraft in keeping their critical flight-refuelling rendezvous and stood-by to co-ordinate SAR in the event of a ditching. The Victor refuelling force was heavily committed to supporting numerous types of sortie and made a few strategic reconnaissance flights over the South Georgia dependency in a temporary reversion to a long-abandoned role.

Rapid re-training of Vulcan crews resulted in use of previously redundant IFR equipment and conventional bombs during world record-breaking long-distance operational sorties, whilst Harriers speedily found their sea legs and their crews mastered new weapons and equipment for combat. The Chinook helicopter — only one of which arrived intact — convincingly demonstrated its usefulness in the army support role, and having lost all their tools and spares, its servicing personnel somehow kept it flying with whatever equipment they could find. When Harriers landed with damage, other ground crew returned them to service employing battle damage repair techniques which reduced down-time from days to hours, or even minutes.

Regrettable though the Falklands war may have been, it was nevertheless an opportunity for Strike Command to prove that its existing procedures were sound and that new practises could be evolved at short notice to meet unusual circumstances. Both tests it passed with ease, whilst simultaneously gaining experience for even more efficient operations in future.

The fundamental lesson for Britain in the Falklands war is that not even the most power-crazed dictator will embark on a military adventure in the certain knowledge of defeat, or even stalemate; if a potential aggressor can be convinced of the existence of effective deterrent forces and the political will to commit them to battle (which Britain failed to do), he will look elsewhere for easier conquests. The South Atlantic campaign served notice to those with designs upon the Western democracies that Britain's armed forces can give a good account of themselves even when outnumbered, and it may be fervently hoped that this demonstration will help to maintain the peace of Europe in years to come.

For as long as there exist powerful forces opposed to the individual freedoms which we take for granted, there will be a requirement for a Strike Command to take its place alongside Britain's other armed Services and those of its allies. Having proven itself in an operation more realistic than any training exercise and grown in stature and experience as a result, the Command can look with fresh confidence to the future, convinced (but more importantly, having convinced others) that there is no idle boast in its motto, 'Defend and Strike'.

A Planner's Nightmare

Operation 'Black Buck 1', the first Vulcan raid on Port Stanley airfield in the early hours of 1 May 1982, required a complex pattern of 18 air-to-air refuellings involving the transfer of 500,000lb (223 tons) of fuel — all 'hook-ups' being made at night. The Vulcan was airborne for over 16 hours and flew some 7,500 miles, achieving a world record for an operational bombing sortie in the process.

Eleven Victors and two Vulcans took part in the outbound waves, of which two Victors and one Vulcan were spares, and in the event, the secondary Vulcan continued with the mission after the primary aircraft developed a pressurisation fault.

The plan's inbuilt flexibility was tested further when the Vulcan was found to be consuming more fuel than anticipated and an unscheduled refuelling was required. The Victor earmarked to make the final pre-target rendezvous then broke its probe whilst taking-on fuel and had to transfer its load to a reserve before returning early to Ascension Island. Following the final transfer, the Victor was left with insufficient fuel to return and a further tanker (not shown) had to be scrambled to meet it. (The Victor pilot refrained from alerting Ascension Island to his predicament until after the Vulcan had dropped its bombs!)

Four Victors comprised the recovery formation, of which two were reserves. A further four Vulcan raids were made on the Falklands, and a fifth was abandoned after five hours when the hose drum unit in the lead Victor failed.

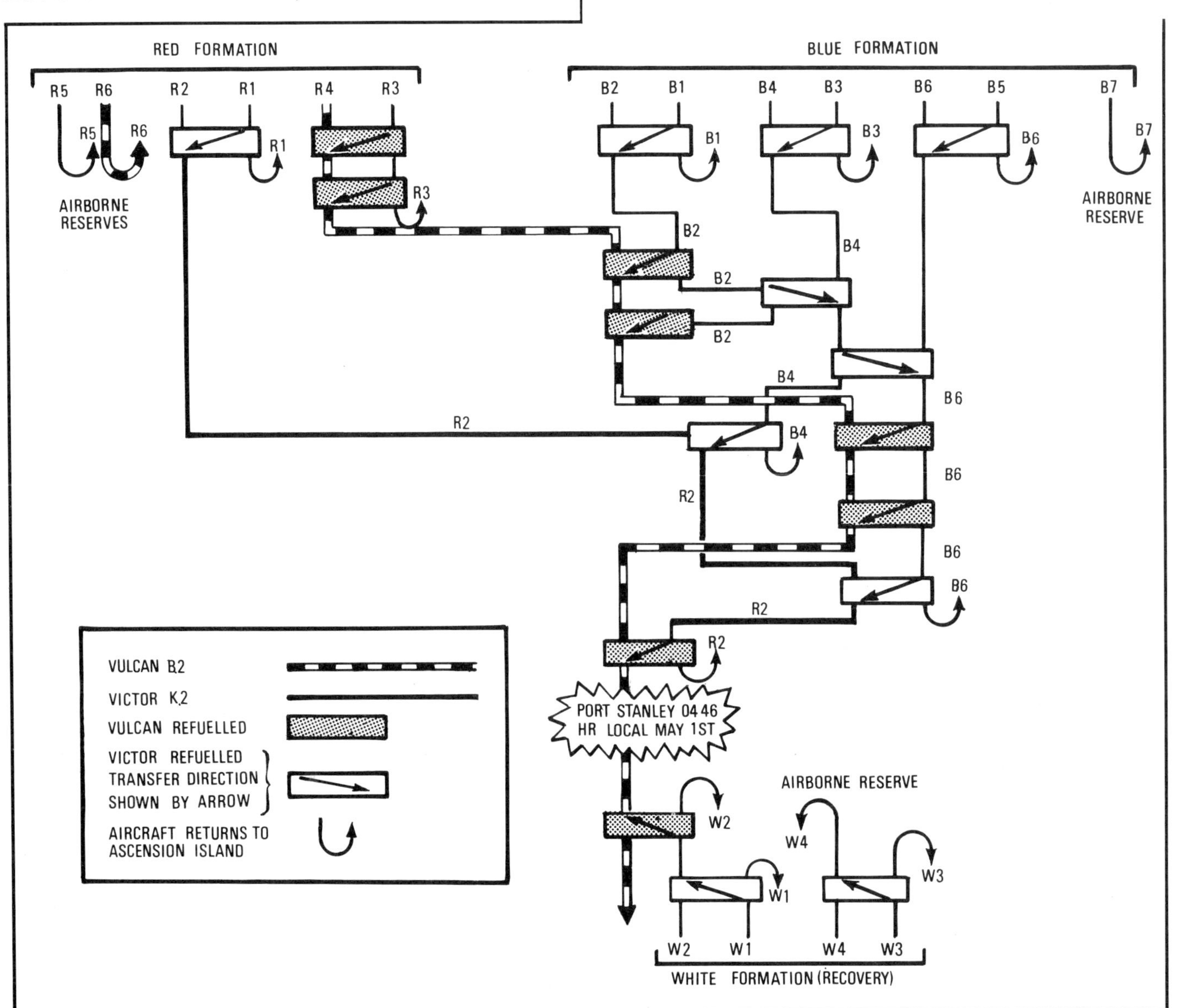